De
A
Cornwall

Atlantic
Ocean

North
Sea

UNITED KINGDOM

R. OF
IRELAND

London

DEVON &
CORNWALL

English Channel

FRANCE

DIAMOND BOOKS

GW00372991

Map of Devon and Cornwall showing:

Atlantic Ocean

English Channel

DEVON
- ILFRACOMBE
- EXMOOR
- BARNSTAPLE
- BIDEFORD
- TIVERTON
- EXETER
- TORQUAY
- PAIGNTON
- BUDE
- DARTMOOR
- TAVISTOCK
- PLYMOUTH

CORNWALL
- BODMIN MOOR
- BODMIN
- PADSTOW
- ST. AUSTELL
- NEWQUAY
- TRURO
- FALMOUTH
- ST. IVES
- PENZANCE
- LAND'S END

The blue section provides you with an alphabetical sequence of headings arranged by county, with Devon, as the larger section, coming first. The headings range through **DEVON-BEACHES** to **CORNWALL-WHAT TO SEE** via **DEVON-EXCURSIONS**, **CORNWALL-RESTAURANTS**, etc. Each entry has information on how to get there, how much it will cost you, when it will be open and what to expect. Furthermore, every page has its own map showing the position of each item and the nearest landmark, allowing you to orientate yourself quickly and easily in your new surroundings. To find what you want to do – having dinner, visiting a museum, going for a walk or shopping for gifts – simply flick through the blue headings and take your pick!

The red section is an alphabetical list of information providing essential facts about the area's main towns and villages, about local culture, and expanding on subjects touched on in the first half of the book. This section also contains practical travel information, such as how to find accommodation, the variety of eating places and food available, information on nightlife, where to find sports and water sports, and the locations of youth hostels. It is lively and informative and easy to use. Each band shows the first three letters of the first entry on the page. Simply flick through the bands till you find the entry you need!

All the main entries are also cross-referenced to help you find them. Names in small capitals – **DEVON-BEACHES 1** – tell you that there is more information about the item you are looking for in the page on beaches in Devon in the first part of the book. So when you read 'see **DEVON-BEACHES 1**' you turn to the blue heading for **DEVON-BEACHES 1**. The instruction 'see **A-Z**' after a word lets you know that the word has its own entry in the second part of the book. Similarly words in bold type – **Mining** – also let you know that there is an entry in the A-Z for the indicated name. In both cases you just look under the appropriate heading in the red section.

CONTENTS

CONTENTS

RED SECTION

INTRODUCTION

n recent years there has been a marked resurgence of interest in domestic holidays, either to replace or to supplement foreign travel. But what are the attractions which await the eight million holiday-makers who travel to Devon and Cornwall each year in search of the great British holiday?

The popular image of a West Country holiday – buckets and spades, cream teas and Cornish pasties – is a double-edged sword for the West Country Tourist Board. After years of holidaying abroad, more sophisticated tourists would not want to be seen dead – even less, buried – on Paignton beach! They certainly would not be impressed by Newquay's cheap, fast-food and trinket-laden High St, and the degree of commercialization of working farms and mines. Yet beyond the more blatant manifestations of tourism is a peaceful, beautiful region that many visitors never see. With two very distinct coastlines, historic cities, picture-postcard rural villages and fishing harbours, unspoiled moors, farm parks, stately homes, a fascinating industrial heritage and a multitude of fine local-museum collections, the variety of things to see and do in Devon and Cornwall is second to none.

The quality of the beaches is the best in Britain and, just to prove it, they consistently win well over 50% of the entire country's total number of Blue Flag awards. Their settings are always varied and often superb, whether a tiny bay sheltered by craggy cliffs, as at Crackington Haven on the north Devon coast, or an endless, golden stretch, such as Praa Sands in south Cornwall. If you enjoy company, go to Torquay or Newquay in July or August, and if you prefer solitude you can usually find a quiet beach away from main resorts out of high season.

All over the region there is a continuing struggle between retaining local character and satisfying the demands of tourism. Many major resorts have lost their individuality, and sadder still, smaller villages and towns such as Mevagissey and Tintagel have sold their souls to the day-tripper. But all is not lost: even places like Torquay, Newquay and Ilfracombe can boast the pretty villages of Cockington, Crantock and Berrynarbor a few minutes from their centres. Towns such as Fowey, Salcombe, Padstow and Sidmouth seem to have struck a happy medium in their tourism development, and in Appledore and Port Isaac you will find villages almost untouched by the holiday trade. Cornwall,

of course, is famous for lovely fishing villages, such as Polperro, Cadgwith and Mousehole, yet the Southwest's archetypal fishing village lies in Devon – Clovelly, which retains its age-old character by banning cars and keeping tourism on a very tight leash. Devon also boasts several idyllic rural villages. The bleak, weather-beaten Dartmoor of *The Hound of the Baskervilles* lies a world away from the beauty of Buckland-in-the-Moor, Widecombe-in-the-Moor and Drewsteignton. Of course, children may be unimpressed by cob and thatch cottages and pretty tea houses but on days when the sun doesn't shine there are plenty of all-weather attractions that will keep them happy and amuse parents at the same time. Farm parks, now an established feature throughout the area, are a good bet for a day out that is both fun and educational. Try the original Milky Way, near Clovelly, the excellent Big Sheep, near Bideford, or Dairyland, near Newquay. Elsewhere there are shire horses to admire, bird and wildlife sanctuaries to visit, caves to explore, steam railways and boat trips to take and theme parks to enjoy. If such obviously staged attractions are not your cup of tea and you don't have children in tow, there are some excellent stately homes and gardens in the region: Cotehele, Lanhydrock and Knightshayes Court are all outstanding, while Castle Drogo and À La Ronde are unique properties. Cornwall is famous for its gardens, and early summer is a gardener's paradise. Trewithen and Trengwainton are nationally acclaimed but non-enthusiasts will take equal pleasure from

the beautifully sited riverside gardens of Trebah (or neighbouring Glendurgan) and Trelissick.

The history of workaday Devon and Cornwall is more fascinating still. Industrial heritage is particularly strong in Cornwall and visible legacies of the tin-mining era are liberally strewn across the landscape. Once-mighty engine houses, now derelict and overgrown, still stand proud – silent witnesses to the centuries when Cornish tin dominated world markets. Less well known is the county's copper-mining history which you can experience in a re-created time capsule at Morwellham Quay. To see more

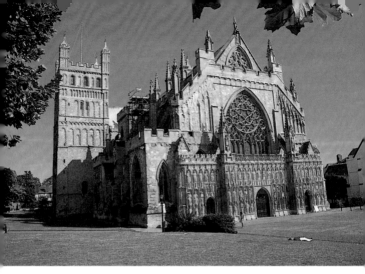

domestic and industrial bygones, simply look in the local museums –
those at Kingsbridge (the Cookworthy Museum), Totnes, Tiverton,
Plymouth, Penzance, Truro and Exeter are all worth a detour, while the
Exeter Maritime Museum is deservedly nationally acclaimed.

The call of the outdoors means a lot more than just sunbathing in this
part of the world. Newquay stages world-class surfing championships
and there are any number of beaches where you can take out a simple
body-board to catch a wave. The extensive programme of ranger-
guided walks on Dartmoor is an ideal introduction to the moors, while
on the coast the well-signposted Southwest Way Coastal Path is equally
accessible and extremely rewarding, even to the reluctant walker.

For lovers of good food and drink the region may not seem quite such
an appetizing prospect. It lacks the choice and quality of eating establishments such a large tourist area should command, but in recent years
several good restaurants have opened, though mostly in the moderate-
expensive price bracket. Pubs and pub food are both disappointing,
often ruined by brewery standardization, although once again there are
notable exceptions if you look hard enough and get off the beaten track.
Shoppers, too, will have to seek interesting local wares away from the

High St and resort mall. Dartington Glass factory is
a favourite day out, while the Cornwall Craft
Association Galleries at Trelowarren, Trelissick and
Pencarrow are probably the best of many fine craft
outlets.

Finally, it is worth reflecting that despite the fleet-
ing fashions of modern-day tourism, Devon and
Cornwall retain an unshakable sense of history –
the enigmatic standing stones of west Cornwall and
the Mayflower Steps at Plymouth, the age-old
Helston Furry Dance and the pagan rites of the
Padstow 'Obby 'Oss, Tintagel's ancient Arthurian
legend and the 18thC *Poldark* saga. The magic of
the Southwest lives on.

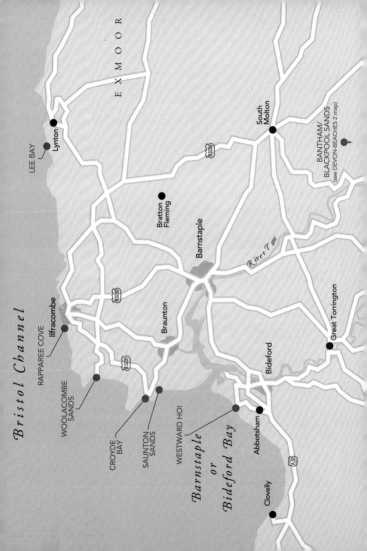

LEE BAY 1 mile west of Lynton.
A picturesque cove which is a sheltered suntrap. Its beach is ideal for family swimming, with gently shelving coarse sand, shingle and pebbles.

RAPPAREE COVE 0.5 miles east of Ilfracombe town centre.
This small cove of gently shelving coarse sand and shingle is flanked by towering cliffs. Good indoor swimming pool adjacent.

WOOLACOMBE SANDS Woolacombe.
The main beach is 400 yd of fine, golden sand backed by grassy dunes but the sands stretch for 2 miles. Popular with families (all amenities) and surfers. Adjacent Barricane Beach is renowned for its shells.

CROYDE BAY Croyde.
Almost a smaller, prettier version of Woolacombe Sands (see above), this fine, flat, soft sandy beach is popular with a similar crowd. Rock pools.

SAUNTON SANDS Saunton.
Three miles of flat, golden sands stretch south from the popular Saunton end, where there are family amenities, surfboard and jet-ski hire, to the near-deserted Braunton Burrows. Bathing is safe except near the river.

WESTWARD HO! Westward Ho!
A long, flat, firm sand-and-pebble beach is backed by a huge pebbly ridge. At high tide the beach is completely covered, so the sands are usually wet. All family amenities; surfboards for hire.

BANTHAM 4 miles west of Kingsbridge.
Wide stretch of gently shelving fine sands in lovely surroundings. Dunes, rock pools and a cliff walk to another good beach at Thurlestone. Shops and pub are a 10-min walk away in Bantham.

BLACKPOOL SANDS 4 miles south of Dartmouth (Blue Flag).
Beautiful wide bay of moderately steep-shelving coarse sand in a verdant setting. Facilities include beach barbecues and a windsurfing school. Popular but not overcommercialized.

ST. MARY'S BAY Brixham.
A popular, 500-yd-long sandy beach backed by cliffs, with rock pools to explore as the tide goes out. Rowing boats for hire.

GOODRINGTON SANDS Paignton (Blue Flag).
Broad, sandy beach with Quaywest and Aquaventure Land, the UK's largest open-air water park. All facilities including water-skiing.

TORRE ABBEY SANDS Torquay (Blue Flag).
This long, wide, fine-red-sand beach is usually wet as it is covered at high tide. Its location makes it very popular, however. Boat hire.

MEADFOOT Torquay (Blue Flag).
A long beach of shingle, sand and pebbles which enjoys a pleasant, natural setting. Rock pools, good swimming, diving and windsurfing.

ANSTEY'S COVE & REDGATE Torquay (Blue Flag).
Two small sun-trap coves, connected by a footbridge and protected by steep cliffs. The beach is either pebbles, sand or shingle. Motorboat hire.

ODDICOMBE Babbacombe, Torquay (Blue Flag).
Amid a picturesque setting of steep, sandstone cliffs topped with lush woodland, a cliff railway descends 240 ft to a steeply shelving long, shingle beach. Boats for hire and speedboat trips.

EXMOUTH Exmouth (Blue Flag).
This 2-mile stretch of golden sand provides fine views across the Exe estuary. Busy but relatively uncommercialized. Rock pools; windsurfing.

BUDLEIGH SALTERTON Budleigh Salterton (Blue Flag).
A quiet, picturesque, 3-mile sweep of shingle and pebbles, dotted with small boats, at the foot of huge, red-sandstone cliffs. Windsurfing.

JACOB'S LADDER Sidmouth (Blue Flag).
A fine, uncommercialized shingle-and-sand beach backed by 500-ft-high cliffs. A whitewashed ladder ascends to peaceful gardens. Boats for hire.

Excursion 1

A one- or two-day excursion from Torquay, visiting classic Dartmoor villages and several attractions. You won't have time to see everything in one day so choose which you would rather visit, or stay overnight on Dartmoor.

Leave Torquay by the A 380 for Newton Abbot, but bypass the town on the A 382 to Bovey Tracey. After 13 miles Parke is signposted to the left on the B 3344.

14 miles – Parke Rare Breeds Farm (see **DEVON-WHAT TO SEE 4**). If you don't visit the farm, you can still admire the beautiful countryside setting and have a coffee here. Continue on the B 3344 to enter Dartmoor proper.

18 miles – Becky Falls. A 70-ft-high waterfall is the central point of an idyllic 60-acre estate set in a thickly wooded valley with crystal streams foaming round huge boulders (1000-1800. Car park £1.50).

19 miles – Manaton. Turn right into the car park, see the 15thC church by the green and come back to the information board which directs you on a short walk to the Bowerman's Nose, a famous face-like rock formation. You can see it away to your left after rejoining the road. Turn right after 0.8 miles down a single-track road.

21.5 miles – North Bovey. This classic village also boasts a 15thC church by its green and, adjacent, the labyrinthine 13thC Ring O' Bells, a low-beamed thatched pub, famous for its food. Continue through the village.

Buckland-in-the-Moor

23.5 miles – Moretonhampstead. This small crossroads town makes a good shopping stop. Cross St is the place for craft shops, while the outstanding Mearsdon Manor Galleries is good for buying and browsing, and for refreshments in its antique tearooms. Take the B 3212 and 2.5 miles from Moretonhampstead you will pass the Miniature Pony Centre (see **DEVON-WHAT TO SEE 4**).

32.5 miles – Postbridge. The medieval stone 'clapper bridge' once used by ponies laden with metal ore, is probably the best example of many such on the moor. The information centre is the starting point for several guided walks (see **Walking**). Backtrack about half a mile and turn right. After 1.8 miles there is a small stone circle to your left. Turn right after another 1.8 miles, then left after a further 2 miles.

40 miles – Widecombe-in-the-Moor (see **A-Z**). Continue through the village towards Buckland. Turn left after 1.5 miles and right after a further 0.7 miles.

43 miles – Buckland-in-the-Moor. Look out for the 'My Dear Mother' clock face just before the picture-postcard thatched cottages. The Roundhouse Craft Centre makes a good break. Continue on through Ashburton, turn right at the first T-junction, left at the next one, then right towards Buckfastleigh.

50 miles – Buckfast Abbey (see **DEVON-WHAT TO SEE 3**).

51 miles – Buckfastleigh Steam Railway and Buckfastleigh Butterfly Farm & Dartmoor Otter Sanctuary (see **DEVON-WHAT TO SEE 3**). These attractions share the same site. Return to Torquay via Newton Abbot by the A 38/383 or alternatively via Totnes on the A 384/385.
Total journey 68 miles.

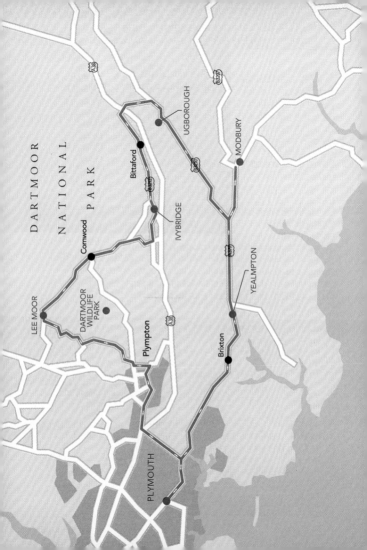

Excursion 2

*A half- or one-day excursion from Plymouth through the beautiful
South Hams and the scenic edge of Dartmoor – equally accessible
from Kingsbridge or Totnes.*

Leave town going east on the ring road and join the A 379. Pass
through Brixton.

7 miles – Yealmpton (pronounced 'Yampton'). The fine main street of
this old village contains the original Old Mother Hubbard's Cottage,
named after the nursery rhyme which was written locally in 1804. It is
now a restaurant. The National Shire Horse Centre is also here (see
DEVON-WHAT TO SEE 3), and you should try to see also 'the most amazing Victorian church in Devon', according to Sir John Betjeman. Pass
through the village.

12 miles – Modbury. The picturesque, steep High St of this small mar-
ket town is full of lovely Georgian shops and houses. Backtrack to the
B 3207, turn right onto it then take the first left (a steep, narrow track).
Turn right at the B 3210 towards Ugborough and Totnes.

15 miles – Ugborough. This large attractive village, built round a
spacious square, boasts a fine medieval church and an unspoiled pub
serving good bar food. Continue on the B 3210, fork left, cross the A 38
and turn left onto the B 3213 (where you pick up the 'Leisure Drive'
signs which you follow as far as Hemerdon Moor). From here to
Ivybridge there are fine views across Dartmoor. Pass through Bittaford.

20.5 miles – Ivybridge. As you pass through this busy small country
town, note the striking Victorian paper mill at the top end. Go past
St. Austin's Priory Church, follow the sign to the Hunting Lodge Pub,
pass under the railway and you will enter the Dartmoor National Park.
Brunel's impressive viaduct stands ahead of you. Go through
Cornwood and onto Lee Moor.

28 miles – Lee Moor. This area is Devon's principal source of kaolin as
evidenced by the white-peaked china-clay slag heaps (see **Mining**). The
views from here southwest to Plymouth are outstanding. Cross
Hemerdon Moor – leave the 'Leisure Drive' unless you want to visit the
Dartmoor Wildlife Park (see **DEVON-WHAT TO SEE 3**) – and return to
Plymouth via Plympton on the B 3416.

Total journey 34 miles.

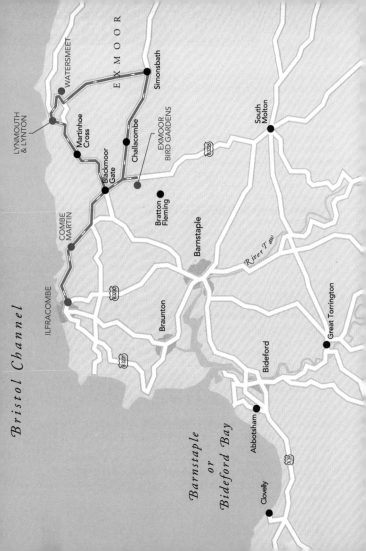

Excursion 3

A one-day excursion from Ilfracombe to the beauty spots of Lynmouth & Lynton, returning via Exmoor.

Leave Ilfracombe going east on the A 399. After 3 miles you will pass Watermouth Bay on your left and the spectacular Watermouth Castle on your right (see **DEVON-WHAT TO SEE 1**, **Berrynarbor**).
6 miles – Combe Martin (see **A-Z**). Stop at the harbour front to admire the bay and perhaps visit the Motorcycle Collection. Go out of the village and after 10 miles turn left at Blackmoor Gate onto the A 39. Pass through Martinhoe Cross and at 17 miles turn left onto the B 3234 and descend sharply.

18 miles – Lynmouth & Lynton (see **A-Z**). Park on the front in Lynmouth, look around, then take the cliff railway up to Lynton. Rejoin the A 39 (heading towards Ilfracombe and Barnstaple).

20 miles – Watersmeet. An idyllic spot for a walk followed by lunch or afternoon tea. After 0.75 miles turn left onto the B 3223. Within a few miles you will experience both rolling greenery and sparse heather hills as you pass along the top of Exmoor (see **A-Z**) at some 1500 ft above sea level. Look out for deer and jaywalking

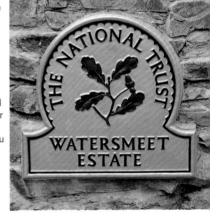

sheep! Turn right at Simonsbath onto the B 3358. Pass through Challacombe and after another 7.5 miles you will come to the B 3226. Turn right to Blackmoor Gate to rejoin the A 399 to return to Ilfracombe 10 miles away or, alternatively, you may wish to make a half-mile diversion here, turning left to Exmoor Bird Gardens (see **DEVON-WHAT TO SEE 1**).
Total journey 40 miles.

BABBACOMBE
FISH & CHIP SHOP

Babbacombe Rd

Babbacombe Rd

West Hill Rd

Marychurch Rd

Lymington Rd

Union St

Newton Rd

Avenue Rd

Shiphay Ave

Maridon Rd

A3022

Torquay Rd

Maridon Rd

Kings Ash Rd

Colley End Rd

Totnes Rd

Penwill Way

Dartmouth Rd

A379

Torquay Rd

Torbay Rd

Belgrave Rd

BOULEVARD

CAPERS

Meadfoot Sea Rd

Ilsham Marine Dr

THE VAULTS

REMY'S/
THE MULBERRY ROOM

Torquay

Paignton

Tor Bay

Restaurants

REMY'S Croft Rd, Torquay, tel: 0803-292359.
❑ 1930-2130 Tue.-Sat. ❑ Expensive.
Remy, the owner and chef, serves classic Gallic cuisine (fresh Brixham fish dishes usually feature) in a delightfully homely atmosphere. Good-value fixed-price menu.

THE VAULTS Victoria Parade, Torquay, tel: 0803-212059.
❑ 1900-2230 Mon.-Sat., & Sun. on BH weekend. ❑ Expensive.
Brick-lined, quarry-tiled vaults provide an informal setting for one of the town's favourite gourmet restaurants. French and international cuisine.

CAPERS Lisburne Sq., off Babbacombe Rd, Torquay, tel: 0803-29117.
❑ 1900-2130 Tue.-Sat. ❑ Expensive.
The inventive and delicious New English menu here makes extensive use of fresh, local produce. Small, elegant dining room. Friendly owners.

THE MULBERRY ROOM Scarborough Rd, Torquay, tel: 0803-213639. ❑ 1000-1700 Wed.-Sun., 1930-2100 Sat. ❑ Moderate.
Lesley Cooper, the owner-chef, serves up excellent wholefood and English dishes (including a Sun. roast) in a charming Victorian parlour which is also Torquay's best tearoom.

BOULEVARD The Pavilion, Seafront, Torquay.
❑ 0930-late. ❑ Inexpensive-Moderate.
Choose from quiches, savoury croissants and a help-yourself salad bar then sit outside on the elegant wrought-iron terrace overlooking the marina. There is also a trendy bistro here.

BABBACOMBE FISH & CHIP SHOP Princes St, off Babbacombe Downs, Torquay, tel: 0803-329928. ❑ 1200-1345, 1700-2300/2330 Mon.-Fri.; 1145-1400, 1700-2330 Sat. ❑ Inexpensive. Takeaways only.
This award-winning chippy is one of the best in the Southwest. Phone ahead to avoid queueing and enjoy the sea views from a bench on Babbacombe Downs!

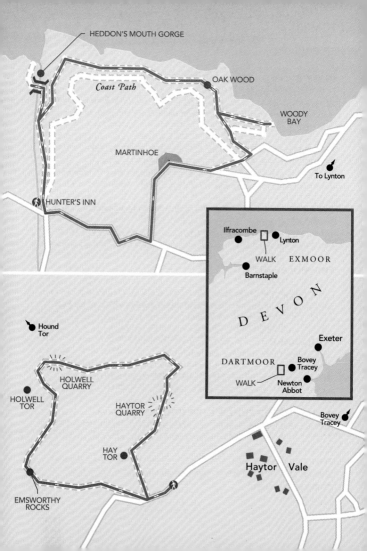

HEDDON'S MOUTH GORGE

Coast Path

OAK WOOD

WOODY BAY

MARTINHOE

To Lynton

HUNTER'S INN

Ilfracombe

Lynton

WALK   EXMOOR

Barnstaple

D E V O N

Hound Tor

Exeter

HOLWELL QUARRY

DARTMOOR

Bovey Tracey

HAYTOR QUARRY

WALK   Newton Abbot

HOLWELL TOR

Bovey Tracey

HAY TOR

Haytor Vale

EMSWORTHY ROCKS

Walks

Heddon's Mouth Gorge on the north Devon coast, near the village of Martinhoe, on Exmoor. 5 miles.
Start from Hunter's Inn, the famous landmark pub. Take the track to the right of the pub towards the coast path. After 50 yd, fork off left away from the coast path. Continue along here and after 250 yd fork left to the spectacular gorge of Heddon's Mouth. Return to the fork and turn left. You can either join the coast path or take a lower path parallel to it. Both give splendid views of the Exmoor coast and its heather-clad slopes. If you take the lower path you will walk through a small, National Trust-owned oak wood. After leaving the trees by the gate a path forks left, running downhill half a mile to Woody Bay, a beautiful, isolated cove, flanked by sandstone cliffs and a breeding ground for seabirds. Come back to the gate and fork right and the path joins a lane. Turn right onto the lane then go straight ahead through a narrow footpath and rejoin the road to the tiny village of Martinhoe. Follow the road around to the left and take the right turn (opposite the telephone box) back to Hunter's Inn.

Haytor Rocks, Dartmoor; near Bovey Tracey in south Devon. 2.5 miles.
Park on the Bovey Tracey-Widecombe-in-the-Moor road (5 miles west of Bovey Tracey) and walk up to Hay Tor. In the Dartmoor vernacular, 'hay' (or 'hey') means high – in this case 1490 ft – and a 'tor' is a pile of rocks. Hay Tor is the most accessible and therefore the most popular of Dartmoor's outcrops. Follow the path in front of the rocks, through the heather to the corner of the wire fence. Here you can pick up the line of the old Haytor Quarry tramlines and descend into the quarry where stone was excavated from the 1820s onwards for such notable struc-tures as London Bridge. The blocks themselves, some 3 to 7 ft long, were laid end-to-end to form the tramroad which was used by horse-drawn trucks. Follow the lines left to the ruined buildings of Holwell Quarry. Climb Holwell Tor and enjoy the view over Houndtor Combe to another famous Dartmoor hill, Hound Tor. Continue round to the left and you will come to two more quarries at Emsworthy Rocks. Just past here a green path leads back to the car park.

What to See 1

EXMOOR BIRD GARDENS Near Bratton Fleming, 8 miles east of Barnstaple. ❑ 1000-1800 April-Oct., 1000-1600 Nov.-Mar. ❑ £3, OAP £2.75, child 3-16 £1.75.
This lovely 12-acre garden is home to over 500 birds and animals, with tropical species, Humboldt penguins, waterfowl and Shetland ponies.

ARLINGTON COURT (NT) 7 miles northeast of Barnstaple.
❑ House 1100-1800 Sun.-Fri., & Sat. on BH weekends, April-Oct. (closes 1700 Oct.). Park dawn-dusk all year.
❑ Garden £2; plus house £4, child 5-17 half price. Disabled.
Former Chichester family home, the house contains fine model ships. The stables house NT's horsedrawn-vehicle collection, with rides in summer.

WATERMOUTH CASTLE 4 miles east of Ilfracombe, tel: 0271-867474. ❑ Sun.-Fri. mid May-mid Sep.; Sun.-Thu. Easter-mid May & mid Sep.-Oct. ❑ £3.90, OAP £3.50, child £2.90.
This theme castle is great fun for all ages, with dancing waters, genuinely scary dungeons, a giant tube slide and lots more. See **Berrynarbor**.

THE BIG SHEEP Abbotsham, 1 mile east of Bideford.
❑ 1000-1800 Easter-Oct. ❑ £2.50, child 4-16 £1.50, family £7.50.
Demonstrations of sheep milking and shearing, sheepdog trialling, spinning and weaving are educational and great fun. Good woollens shop.

DARTINGTON CRYSTAL Great Torrington.
❑ Glass centre 0900-1700 Mon.-Fri., plus 1000-1630 Sat., Sun., late July-Aug. Factory tours 0930-1530 Mon.-Fri. (1630 mid July-early Sep.).
❑ Glass centre 75p, child 6-16 25p, plus tour £1.40, child 70p.
A fascinating opportunity to watch the highly skilled production techniques of crystal-glass craftsmen (see the video before the factory tour).

THE MILKY WAY 2 miles south of Clovelly.
❑ 1200-1800 Sun.-Fri. ❑ £2.50, OAP £2, child 3-16 £1.50.
Longest-established of the many working dairy farms opened to the public in the region, and voted Britain's best open farm for 1990. Everyone gets a go at bottle-feeding and hand-milking.

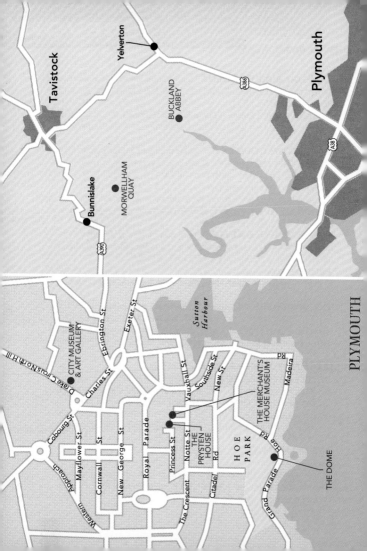

THE DOME The Hoe, Plymouth.
❑ 1000-2030 (last entry 1900) July-Sep.; 1000-1830 Mon.-Fri., 1000-2030 Sat., Sun. & BH Easter-June; 1000-1830 Oct.-Easter.
❑ July-Sep. £2.50, OAP £2, child 5+ £1.65, family £7. Other times £2.10, OAP £1.85, child £1.45, family £7.
The best in audio-visual technology takes you back through Elizabethan Plymouth, great sea voyages, Civil War, Victorian Empire and the Blitz. A high-tech observation area lets you zoom in on ships in Plymouth Sound.

THE MERCHANT'S HOUSE MUSEUM St. Andrew's St, Plymouth. ❑ 1000-1730 Tue.-Sat., 1400-1700 Sun., 1000-1300, 1400-1700 BH Mon. ❑ 65p, child 15p.
Entertaining history displays in this 16thC house depict themed tinker, tailor, soldier, sailor, etc. plus a fully stocked apothecary's shop.

THE PRYSTEN HOUSE (Yogges House) Finewell St, Plymouth.
❑ 1000-1700 Easter-Oct. ❑ 50p, OAP/child 5-13 25p.
The oldest house in Plymouth, built in 1498. This atmospheric architectural gem has been a merchant's home and a monks' meeting place.

CITY MUSEUM & ART GALLERY Drake Circus, Plymouth.
❑ 1000-1730 Tue.-Sat., 1400-1700 Sun., 1000-1700 BH Mon. ❑ Free.
An outstanding collection of fine and decorative arts. Exhibitions.

MORWELLHAM QUAY 5 miles southeast of Tavistock.
❑ 1000-1730 (last entry 1530) Mar.-Oct.; 1000-1630 (1430) Nov.-Feb. (closed Christmas week). ❑ £4.90, OAP £4.25, child £3.40.
*Marvellous recreation of life in a bustling copper-mining port c.1868, with a 'tram' ride deep into a copper mine. See **A-Z**.*

BUCKLAND ABBEY (NT) Nr Yelverton, 6 miles south of Tavistock.
❑ 1030-1730 Fri.-Wed., April-Oct. (1700 Oct.); 1400-1700 Sat., Sun., Nov.-Mar. ❑ Grounds £1.60; plus house £3.60, child 5-17 half price.
Majestic abbey, converted to a mansion in the 1570s and sold to Francis Drake. Few medieval parts remain after a fire in 1938. The fine Drake Gallery contains his legendary drum. 14thC tithe barn; craft workshops.

SALTRAM HOUSE (NT) Plympton, 2 miles west of Plymouth.
❏ House 1230-1800, art gallery, garden & great kitchen 1100-1800 Sun.-Thu. (also Sat. on BH weekends), April-Oct. (all close 1700 Oct.).
❏ Garden £1.60; plus house, etc. £4.40, child 5-17 half price. Car park 50p (Sun. only). Disabled (partly).
A splendid mid-18thC mansion boasting flamboyant Robert Adam decoration, portraits by Reynolds and sumptuous furnishings.

NATIONAL SHIRE HORSE CENTRE Yealmpton, near Plymouth.
❏ 1000-1700. Parades 1130, 1430, 1615. No parades mid Nov.-mid Mar.; nominal entrance fee. ❏ £3.95, OAP £3.50, child £2.75.
Over 40 giant Shires parade and show off carriage-manoeuvring skills. Stables, forge and museum plus birds of prey show and butterfly centre.

DARTMOOR WILDLIFE PARK Sparkwell, 9 miles east of Plymouth. ❏ 1000-dusk. ❏ £3.95, OAP £3.20, child 4-14 £2.75.
Big cats, bison and bears are among the 150 species at this beautifully sited park. 'Close encounters' for children; falconry displays Sat.-Thu.

BUCKFAST ABBEY Buckfastleigh.
❏ 0530-2100. ❏ Free. Car park 75p.
A rare example of a living Benedictine monastery church, remarkably built by just a few monks between 1907-37. An exhibition relates the abbey's history and the way of life for today's monks.

BUCKFASTLEIGH BUTTERFLY FARM & DARTMOOR OTTER SANCTUARY Buckfastleigh Station. ❏ 1000-1730 or dusk. Butterfly Farm mid Mar-mid Nov., Otter Sanctuary Mar-mid Dec.
❏ Joint admission £2.75, OAP £2.20, child £1.50.
Brilliantly coloured butterflies and giant moths flutter by you in a steamy hothouse. The playful otters will delight all the family.

BUCKFASTLEIGH STEAM RAILWAY Buckfastleigh Station.
❏ 3-4 trips per day; 25 min per trip. ❏ From £4.30, child £3.
A nostalgic ride along the old Great Western Railway route following the picturesque River Dart. Railway museum and model railway at station.

M5

M5

A396

A396

A361

A3072

A30

A382

A30

A386

A3121

A376

A380

A379

Sidmouth

Budleigh Salterton

Exmouth

Broadclyst

Tiverton

THE BRUNEL ATMOSPHERIC RAILWAY

POWDERHAM CASTLE

Kenton

Exeter

CASTLE DROGO

Moretonhampstead

Bovey Tracey

PARKE RARE BREEDS FARM

South Molton

MINIATURE PONY CENTRE

DARTMOOR

LYDFORD GORGE

Great Torrington

PARKE RARE BREEDS FARM 0.5 miles west of Bovey Tracey.
❑ 1000-1800 April-Oct. ❑ £2.75, OAP £2.50, child £1.50.
*The only nationally approved rare-breeds farm in the West Country, Parke
holds exotic varieties of every type of farmyard animal. Interpretation
Centre and beautiful woodland and river walks. See* **DEVON-EXCURSION 1***.*

MINIATURE PONY CENTRE 3 miles west of Moretonhampstead.
❑ 1000-1800 April-Sep., 1100-1700 Mar., Oct. ❑ £3, OAP £2.50,
child 3+ £2. Pony rides 50p each.
*Young children will love the Shetland ponies in this panoramic moor set-
ting. Pygmy cattle, goats, rabbits and donkeys continue the tiny theme.*

POWDERHAM CASTLE Kenton, 5 miles south of Exeter.
❑ 1400-1730 Sun.-Thu., Spring BH-mid Sep. ❑ £2.75, child £1.75.
*Seat of the Earls of Devon for 600 years, Powderham boasts rich
Georgian interiors, handsome halls, a fine chapel plus a deer park.*

THE BRUNEL ATMOSPHERIC RAILWAY Starcross.
❑ 1000-1800 Mon.-Sat., 1415-1800 Sun. ❑ £1.90, OAP £1.60,
child 90p, family £4.90.
*Interesting exhibition in an old pumping station, explaining an ingenious
19thC system of railway propulsion by Brunel. Fine views from the top.*

LYDFORD GORGE (NT) Main entrance 1 mile south of Lydford,
second entrance 2 miles south of Lydford. ❑ 1030-1800 April-Oct.,
1030-1600 Nov.-April. ❑ £2.20, child 5-17 half price.
*Walk along a steep, wooded valley with bubbling waters swirling through
a succession of potholes, to the thundering whirlpool of Devil's Cauldron
at one end and the peaceful 90-ft-high White Lady Waterfall at the other.*

CASTLE DROGO (NT) Near Drewsteignton.
❑ 1100-1800 Sat.-Thu., April-Oct. (closes 1700 Oct.) ❑ Garden £1.60;
plus house £3.80, child 5-17 half price. Disabled.
*This forbidding-looking bare-granite country house was designed by
Lutyens (1911-30) and is the last castle built in England. It is unique and
full of interest. Wonderful views. Play croquet in the grounds.*

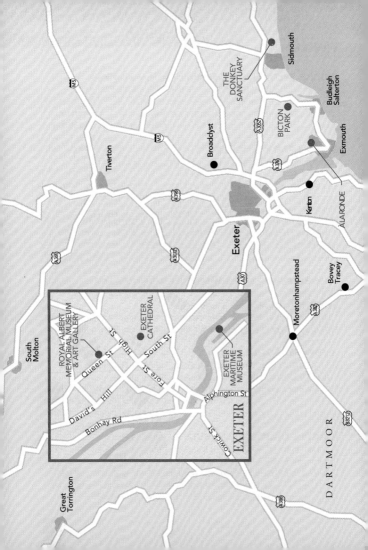

THE DONKEY SANCTUARY Near Salcombe Regis.
❏ 0900-dusk. ❏ Free.
The country's largest donkey haven is home to an incredible 4500 animals. See the happy rescued and revived animals in their barns and paddocks or walk round the farmyard and fields.

BICTON PARK East Budleigh.
❏ 1000-1800 April-Oct. ❏ £3.25, OAP £2.75 (Wed., Thu. £2), child 3+ £2. Children's attractions 50p-£1 each.
60 acres of beautifully landscaped formal and informal gardens include glasshouses, a good countryside museum and various children's rides.

À LA RONDE Summer Lane, 1.5 miles north of Exmouth.
❏ 1000-1700 Mon.-Sat., plus 1100-1800 Sun., Easter-Oct. ❏ £2.50, child £1. Disabled.
A highly entertaining 1-hr tour will show you a multitude of curiosities, unique shell and feather wall decorations and the many secrets of this intriguing 16-sided, 20-roomed 18thC folly.

EXETER CATHEDRAL Exeter.
One of England's finest churches, boasting two unique Norman transept towers and a striking, sculpted West Front. With huge Gothic vaulting, a splendid 15thC clock and several medieval monuments.

ROYAL ALBERT MEMORIAL MUSEUM & ART GALLERY
Queen St, Exeter. ❏ 1000-1730 Tue.-Sat. ❏ Free.
East Devon's largest and best general-interest museum features an excellent ethnography section plus natural history, timepieces and local silverware.

EXETER MARITIME MUSEUM The Quay, Exeter.
❏ 1000-1700 Sep.-June, 1000-1800 July, Aug. ❏ £3, OAP £2.50, child £1.75, family £8.50.
A wonderful collection of around 100 working boats from all over the world, either afloat (some may be boarded), or in the 19thC warehouses. Good, informative displays; children's activity area.

KILLERTON HOUSE (NT) Broadclyst, 7 miles north of Exeter.
❑ Park & garden dawn-dusk daily. House 1100-1800 Wed.-Mon.,
April-Oct. (closes 1700 Oct.). ❑ Garden £2.20 (£1 winter); plus house
£3.60, child 5-17 half price. Disabled (partly).
*Beautiful sweeping hillside gardens and landscaped grounds provide
elegant walking. The light, airy 18thC house features the excellent NT
Costume Collection, displaying 18th-20thC garments.*

BICKLEIGH MILL ('Devonshire's Centre') Bickleigh.
❑ 1000-1800 April-Oct., 1000-1700 Nov., Dec.; Sat., Sun. only, Jan.-
Mar. ❑ £3, child 4-13 £2.
*Craft workshops around a restored mill and water wheel form the
nucleus of this family attraction. Motor centre, farm animals, otters and
bird enclosures plus a children's play area.*

BICKLEIGH CASTLE 9 miles north of Exeter.
❑ 1400-1700 Easter week; Wed., Sun., BHs up to Spring BH; Sun.-Fri.
Spring BH-early Oct. ❑ £2.20, child 5-15 £1.10. Disabled.
*Romantic moated and fortified manor house with 11thC chapel, great
hall and intriguing collection of World War II spying and escape gadgets.*

KNIGHTSHAYES COURT (NT) 2 miles north of Tiverton.
❑ Garden 1100-1800 daily; house 1330-1800 Sat.-Thu., April-Oct.
(closes 1700 Oct.). Disabled. ❑ Garden £2.20; plus house £4.
*Splendid light and airy 19thC Gothic Revival house with 18th and 19thC
English furniture and rich Pre-Raphaelite decor. Beautiful grounds.*

QUINCE HONEY FARM North Rd, South Molton.
❑ 0900-1800 (1700 Nov.-Easter). ❑ £2.45, OAP £2, child 5-16 £1.10.
*The world's largest apiary extravaganza, featuring 20 beehive displays
and a million honey bees. Children love it. Picnic area and honey shop.*

COLDHARBOUR MILL Uffculme, 11 miles east of Tiverton.
❑ 1100-1700 (last tour 1600) Easter-Oct. ❑ £2.75.
*Working mill museum which has produced textiles since 1797. The tour
shows you huge steam engines, and spinning and weaving machinery.*

MODEL VILLAGE

BYGONES

KENT'S
CAVERN

Babbacombe Rd

Ilsham Dr

Meadfoot Sea Rd

Babbacombe Rd

Marychurch Rd

West Hill Rd

Lymington Rd

Union St

Belgrave Rd

Newton Rd

Avenue Rd

TORRE
ABBEY

Shiphay Ave

Marldon Rd

Torquay Rd

A3022

Torquay Rd

Maridon Rd

Kings Ash Rd

Colley End Rd

Totnes Rd

Penwill Way

PAIGNTON
ZOO

Torbay Rd

Torbay Rd

A379

Dartmouth Rd

PAIGNTON-KINGSWEAR
STEAM RAILWAY

Torquay

Paignton

Tor Bay

MODEL VILLAGE Babbacombe, Torquay.
☐ 0900-2200 Easter-Sep., 0900-2100 1 Oct.-mid Oct., 0900-1700 mid Oct.-Easter. ☐ £2.50, child £1.50.
This outstanding model village, full of interest and with a fine sense of humour, is a masterpiece of miniature landscape gardening. By day a riot of natural colour, by night brilliantly illuminated.

BYGONES Fore St, St. Marychurch, Torquay.
☐ 1000-'late' June-Sep., 1000-1700 Oct.-May. ☐ £1.75, child 5-15 £1.
A realistic, colourful, life-size recreation of a Victorian street plus rooms above. The attention to nostalgic detail even includes authentic smells.

KENT'S CAVERN Wellswood, off Babbacombe Rd, Torquay.
☐ 1000-1800 April-June, Sep., Oct.; 1000-2100 July, Aug. (closes 1800 Sat.); 1000-1700 Nov.-Mar. ☐ £2.30, child 5-15 £1.30.
This fascinating and atmospheric guided tour of one of Europe's most important ancient sites takes you back 500,000 years, through spectacular rock formations and prehistoric remains.

TORRE ABBEY Torbay Rd, Torquay.
☐ 1000-1900 (Palm House 0900-1545) April-Oct. ☐ £1.50, OAP/child 8-15 75p, family £3.50.
Part 12thC monastery, part 16thC mansion, the 'abbey' is an interesting mix of stately home, art gallery, local museum (with an Agatha Christie room), monastery ruins and exotic gardens.

PAIGNTON ZOO Totnes Rd, Paignton.
☐ 1000-1830. ☐ £3.95, OAP £3.20, student/child 3-14 £2.60.
One of England's largest zoos set amid 75 acres of lawns and gardens. Elephants, rhinos, lions, tigers, monkeys and giraffes vie to steal the show.

PAIGNTON-KINGSWEAR STEAM RAILWAY (Dart Valley Railway) Station Sq., Paignton. ☐ 4-9 trains per day. ☐ £4.30.
A splendid, scenic, 7-mile trip along the Torbay coast, stopping at Goodrington Sands and Churston, then down through the wooded slopes of the glorious Dart estuary to Kingswear.

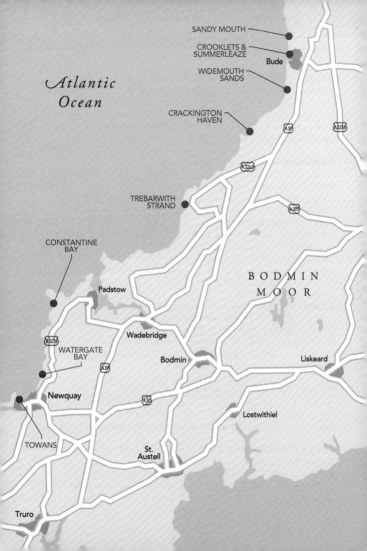

SANDY MOUTH

CROOKLETS & SUMMERLEAZE

Bude

WIDEMOUTH SANDS

CRACKINGTON HAVEN

A39

A3254

A3263

Atlantic Ocean

A395

TREBARWITH STRAND

B O D M I N M O O R

CONSTANTINE BAY

Padstow

B3276

Wadebridge

Liskeard

WATERGATE BAY

A39

Bodmin

Newquay

A30

Lostwithiel

TOWANS

Truro

St. Austell

SANDY MOUTH 3 miles north of Bude.
A pleasant beach of moderately shelving sand and pebbles, sheltered on three sides by cliffs. Amenities include a good NT café.

CROOKLETS & SUMMERLEAZE Bude.
Crooklets to the north has been called Britain's Bondi and is Bude's main surfing and swimming beach, while large, sandy Summerleaze is popular with families.

WIDEMOUTH SANDS 3 miles south of Bude.
The main beach of this pleasant, sandy bay stretches 300 yd and is popular with surfers and families. All amenities.

CRACKINGTON HAVEN 12 miles south of Bude (via A 39).
This small cove of sand and pebbles is set picturesquely between a sheer cliff and green hills. Good for surfing and with excellent, if steep, cliff walks. Shops and hotel adjacent.

TREBARWITH STRAND 2 miles south of Tintagel.
This popular fine-sand beach is approached through a delightful wooded valley. With a surf school, good pub and two fine café/restaurants.

CONSTANTINE BAY 4 miles west of Padstow.
A long, wide, sweeping arc of moderately shelving soft sands continues intermittently from Booby's Bay to Treyarnon Bay. The latter is the most sheltered and popular and has some facilities.

WATERGATE BAY 3 miles north of Newquay.
Two miles of fine, flat, golden sand backed by cliffs rising to 200 ft, though these give little shelter. Hotel, beach shop/café, wet suits and surfboard hire. Good cliff walks.

TOWANS Newquay.
The most popular of Newquay's beaches – flat, firm, golden sands stretch from the harbour to spectacular cliffs, joined to one another by a small suspension bridge. All amenities.

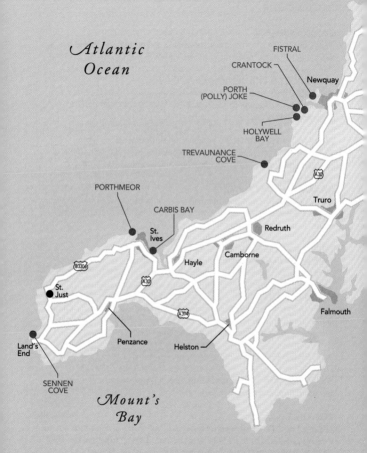

FISTRAL Newquay.
This is the largest and, as it faces west, the sunniest of the Newquay beaches. Atlantic rollers make it a mecca for surfers but strong currents can make swimming hazardous. Board hire; snack facilities on beach.

CRANTOCK 3 miles south of Newquay.
Excellent large, flat, sandy beach backed by high dunes and rolling grasslands. Piper's Hole cave can be explored at low tide. Beware estuary currents. Café/beach shop hires surfboards. Good pub in village.

PORTH (POLLY) JOKE West Pentire, 4 miles west of Newquay.
This beach, a 10-15 min walk from the car park, is the best unspoiled, sandy beach close to Newquay. One café.

HOLYWELL BAY 4 miles south of Newquay.
This half-mile of golden sands backed by grassy dunes and low, green cliffs is very popular with families and has been highly commercialized to include a leisure park. Surfing only at high tide.

TREVAUNANCE COVE 0.5 miles north of St. Agnes.
A good sandy beach in a rocky cove, hemmed in by steep cliffs. Very popular with surfers. Watch them and the local gliders above from the Bistro beach café.

CARBIS BAY 1 mile southeast of St. Ives.
Steep, verdant hillsides provide a beautiful setting for this excellent long, wide family beach, boasting some of Cornwall's best sands. All amenities including water-skiing and windsurfing.

PORTHMEOR St. Ives (Blue Flag).
Lovely half-mile length of golden sand is St. Ives' most popular beach, especially with surfers. Small promenade with café, shop and board hire.

SENNEN COVE Whitesand Bay, near Land's End (Blue Flag).
Silvery sands stretch for a mile from Sennen Cove harbour, forming one of Cornwall's most attractive long beaches. Good for experienced surfers.

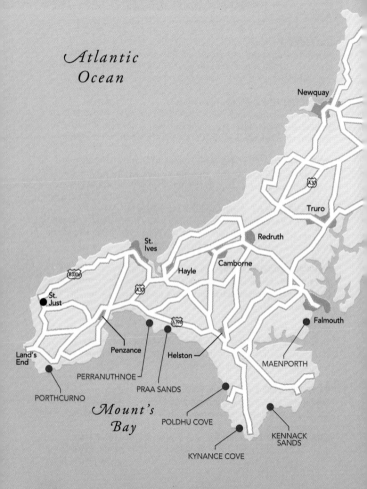

Atlantic
Ocean

Newquay

A30

Truro

Redruth

St.
Ives

Camborne

B3306

Hayle

A30

St.
Just

A394

Falmouth

Land's
End

Penzance

Helston

MAENPORTH

PORTHCURNO

PERRANUTHNOE

PRAA SANDS

Mount's
Bay

POLDHU COVE

KYNANCE COVE

KENNACK
SANDS

PORTHCURNO 7.5 miles west of Penzance.
This picturesque half-mile-long bay of steeply shelving fine, white sand is dotted with tiny coves between rocky outcrops. Snacks available in the car park.

PERRANUTHNOE Perran Sands, 4 miles east of Penzance.
The best beach close to Penzance – the gently shelving shingle and sand here make the waters ideal for swimming. Snacks on the beach; good pub and shop in the village.

PRAA SANDS 5 miles west of Helston.
This mile-long crescent of firm, gently shelving fine golden sand is the area's most popular beach. Low water reveals rock pools at each end. All facilities including diving, surfing and windsurfing.

POLDHU COVE 1 mile west of Mullion.
An easily accessible, popular sandy cove, favoured by surfers. Café and a beach shop. Footpaths lead to the quieter beaches at Church Cove and Dollar Cove.

KYNANCE COVE 11 miles south of Helston.
This classic cove is famous for the towering cliffs and rock formations overlooking its white-gold sands (try to arrive before low water). Very popular despite its relative isolation. Beach café.

KENNACK SANDS 9 miles south of Helston.
A fine 500-yd-long sandy crescent is exposed at high tide and is ideal for swimming. Unspoiled but can get crowded. Cafés, beach shop and surf-board hire.

MAENPORTH 3 miles south of Falmouth.
This small, attractive, sheltered beach of gently shelving firm sand is bounded by low cliffs and rock pools. All facilities, including scuba and windsurfing schools.

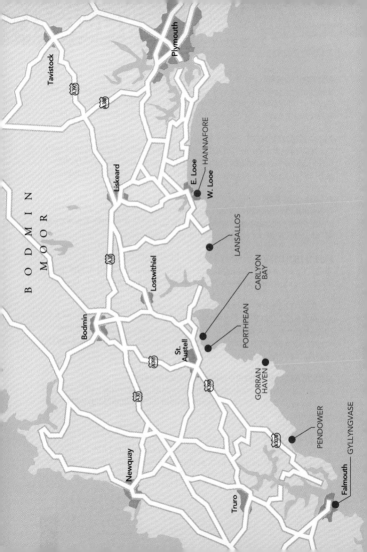

GYLLYNGVASE Falmouth.
The most popular of Falmouth's beaches, this long stretch of coarse sand and shingle is ideal for family bathing. All facilities on the seafront including windsurfing and water-ski schools, plus jet-ski hire (parascending at adjacent Swanpool beach).

PENDOWER (Carne) 1 mile southwest of Veryan.
A fine, unspoiled, mile-long strip of coarse sand with moderately shelving shingle, ideal for safe bathing. Rock pools for children, windsurfing, water-skiing and canoeing, plus hotel beer garden.

GORRAN HAVEN Gorran Haven.
This quiet resort boasts a good, safe, sandy beach for swimming. Shops, cafés and boat hire.

PORTHPEAN St. Austell.
This popular small suntrap bay of coarse sand and shingle can get rather crowded. Rock pools for the kids, café/beach shop and boat hire.

CARLYON BAY Crinnis Beach, St. Austell.
Over a mile of sheltered, sandy bays and beaches, including access to Polgaver Bay, Cornwall's only official naturist beach. Highly commercialized area, with a leisure centre offering all facilities including water-skiing.

LANSALLOS West Combe, 3 miles west of Polperro.
15 min walk from Lansallos Church.
This small, sandy cove overlooked by tall cliffs is completely natural and usually quiet. There are good rock pools and seals can sometimes be spotted offshore.

HANNAFORE (West Looe) 1 mile west of Looe.
Shingle, rocks (with good rock pools) and sandy patches make up the beach here. Café and beach shop. For more sand and fewer people, walk 10 min along the cliff path to Portnadler Bay.

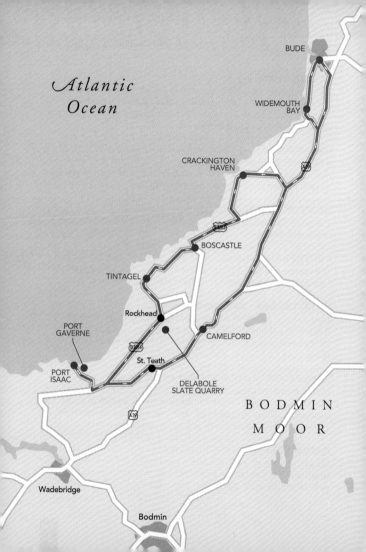

Excursion

A one-day excursion around the rugged and spectacular north Cornwall coast, starting from Bude. Fri. is market day in Camelford. Do the tour anti-clockwise if you want to visit the beaches in the afternoon.

Leave Bude on the coast road heading south.

3 miles – Widemouth Bay (see **CORNWALL-BEACHES 1**). At the far end of the bay follow the road inland and turn right on to the A 39. After 3 miles turn right.

6 miles – Crackington Haven. This spectacular spot is worth a visit regardless of its beach (see **CORNWALL-BEACHES 1**). Follow the steep hill until you come to the B 3263, then turn right.

12.75 miles – Boscastle (see **A-Z**). Park your car and walk along by the river down to the much-photographed harbour. There are several refreshment possibilities here. Continue on the B 3263.

15.75 miles – Tintagel (see **A-Z**). The legendary seat of King Arthur, see 'his' Great Hall, the supposed site of his castle and The Old Post Office. Continue on the B 3263 through Trewarmett. Take the second on the right up the steep hill, then turn left towards Rockhead. Turn right on to the B 3314 and look for a small sign on the left.

27 miles – Delabole Slate Quarry. A public viewing point (free) allows you a vertiginous stare into one of the biggest man-made holes in Europe. Continue on the B 3314 for 5 miles. Turn right just past The Cornish Arms.

33 miles – Port Gaverne. This small cove is an appetizer for Port Isaac. If you can park here then do so and walk the mile to Port Isaac.

34 miles – Port Isaac (see **A-Z**). The steep, narrow alleys of this unspoiled port ooze character. Backtrack left on to the B 3314 and after 0.25 miles turn right on to the B 3267 to St. Teath. Pass through St. Teath and turn left on to the A 39.

41.25 miles – Camelford. This small roadside town is worth a stop for its fine North Cornwall Museum & Gallery (1030-1700 Mon.-Sat., April-Sep. £1, concessions 75p, child 50p). Continue on the A 39 back to Bude.

Total journey 57 miles.

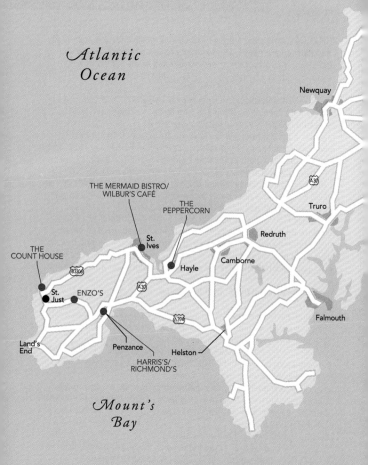

Atlantic
Ocean

Newquay

THE MERMAID BISTRO/
WILBUR'S CAFÉ

THE
PEPPERCORN

A30

Truro

St.
Ives

Redruth

THE
COUNT HOUSE

B3306

Hayle

Camborne

A30

St.
Just

ENZO'S

Falmouth

Land's
End

A394

Penzance

Helston

HARRIS'S/
RICHMOND'S

Mount's
Bay

Restaurants

THE COUNT HOUSE Botallack, 1 mile north of St. Just, tel: 0736-788588. ❏ 1930-2200 Tue.-Sat., 1230-1345 Sun. ❏ Expensive.
Imaginative, mouthwatering New English dishes are served by a charming husband-and-wife team in a lovely converted barn.

HARRIS'S 46 New St, Penzance, tel: 0736-64408.
❏ 1200-1400 Tue.-Sat., 1900-2200 Mon.-Sat. ❏ Expensive.
The menu here is short but the delicious food is consistently rated Penzance's finest, with steaks in sauces and inventive fish dishes.

ENZO'S Newbridge, tel: 0736-63777.
❏ 1900-2130 Mon.-Sat., 1900-2100 Sun. ❏ Moderate-Expensive.
Book a table in the delightful conservatory here – a mini-jungle relieved by gingham tablecloths and terracotta. Both antipasto and sweet trollies are splendid and the open kitchen serves inventive Italian dishes.

THE MERMAID BISTRO Fish St, St. Ives, tel: 0736-796816.
❏ 1830-2200 Mon.-Sat. ❏ Moderate-Expensive.
This charming former fisherman's cottage and sail loft serves excellent fresh local fish dishes plus a good range of international specialities.

THE PEPPERCORN Fore St, Hayle, tel: 0736-752001.
❏ 1900-late Tue.-Sun. ❏ Moderate.
This attractive small bistro run by a Spanish chef and his wife serves an excellent variety of 'French peasant' and international dishes, using local fresh produce. Tapas on Sun.

RICHMOND'S Chapel St, Penzance, tel: 0736-63540.
❏ 1030-1700, 1830-2230. ❏ Moderate.
An ideal place at any time, from morning coffee with delicious cakes to an extensive menu of pasta, steak and seafood. Everything home-cooked.

WILBUR'S CAFÉ St. Andrew's St, St. Ives, tel: 0736-796661.
❏ 1830-late. ❏ Inexpensive-Moderate.
Stylish burger and steaks restaurant, decorated with old photos, pot plants and nostalgic memorabilia. Good, lively atmosphere.

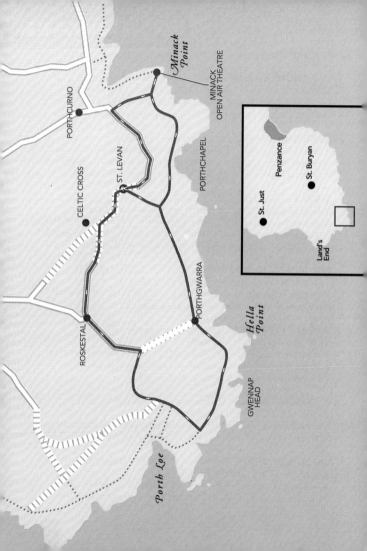

Minack Point

MINACK
OPEN AIR THEATRE

PORTHCURNO

CELTIC CROSS

ST. LEVAN

PORTHCHAPEL

ROSKESTAL

PORTHGWARRA

Hella Point

GWENNAP
HEAD

Porth Loe

Penzance

St. Buryan

St. Just

Land's
End

Porthgwarra and Gwennap Head, 3 miles south of Land's End.
A moderately easy walk along the Cornish Coastal Path. 4 miles.
Park by St. Levan Church, named after a 5th or 6thC Celtic saint. The present building is mainly 13th-15thC and is worth a look inside. Turn left at the end of the road, walk uphill and you will see a Celtic Cross. Turn left here and you will come to the hamlet of Roskestal. Follow the road left to Porthgwarra. After about three quarters of a mile take the second right turn (the first is a short path leading to a dead end). This

leads downhill, across a stream and past the coast-guard station to the coastal footpath. Follow this round to the left to be rewarded with some of Cornwall's finest cliff scenery, looking out to Gwennap Head. Walk through Porthgwarra and skirt the small, sandy beach of Porthchapel. From here you can return to St. Levan or continue a little further to Porthcurno to view its lovely beach (see **CORNWALL-BEACHES 3**) and, high above on the cliffs, the precariously perched Minack Open Air Theatre (see **Theatre**). It has been staging plays since 1932 and must surely have the most dramatic setting of any open-air theatre in the country. Then walk back on the road to St. Levan.

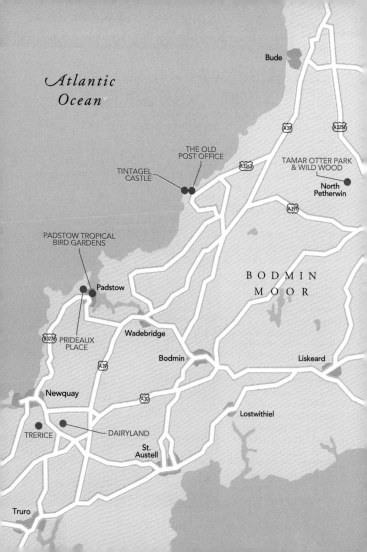

What to See 1

TINTAGEL CASTLE (EH) Tintagel, tel: 0840-770328.
❏ 1000-1800 Easter-Sep.; 1000-1600 Tue.-Sun., Oct.-Easter. Landrover
25p, or 0.5 mile steep walk. ❏ £1.60, OAP £1.20, child 5-16 80p.
*There is disappointingly little to see of the legendary seat of King Arthur
but the stupendous setting and views make the trek worthwhile.*

THE OLD POST OFFICE (NT) Tintagel.
❏ 1100-1800 Apr.-Oct. (1700 Oct.). ❏ £1.60, child 5-17 80p. Dis. (part).
*Tiny 14thC manor house functioned as the village post office, 1844-92.
Its post room, hall, parlour and bedrooms have been charmingly restored.*

PADSTOW TROPICAL BIRD GARDENS Fentonluna Lane,
Padstow, tel: 0841-532262. ❏ 1030-2000 (last entry 1900) summer,
1030-1700 (last entry 1600) winter. ❏ £2.75, OAP £2, child 4-16 £1.45.
*Two acres of beautifully landscaped gardens with exotic, tropical birds in
aviaries and the outstanding Butterfly World in a steamy hothouse.*

PRIDEAUX PLACE Tregirl Lane, Padstow.
❏ 1330-1700 Easter fortnight, 1100-1700 Sun.-Thu., Spring BH-Sep.
❏ £2.50, child £1.
An interesting mix of Tudor, Georgian and Gothic in 16thC manor house.

DAIRYLAND 4 miles south of Newquay.
❏ 1030-1730 Easter, May-Sep.; 1200-1700 April, Oct. & Sat. in low
season. ❏ £3.50, OAP £3, child 4-15 £2.
Working farm with milking parlour and excellent country-life museum.

TRERICE (NT) 3 miles south of Newquay.
❏ 1100-1800 April-Oct. (closes 1700 Oct.). ❏ £3.20, child 5-17 half
price. Disabled (partly).
Delightful small Elizabethan manor house set in a wooded valley.

TAMAR OTTER PARK & WILD WOOD North Petherwin.
❏ 1030-1800 April-Oct. ❏ £2.50, OAP £2, child £1.50.
*Five enclosures hold British and Asian otters but the real stars are the
tame free-roaming deer and muntjac in the 'wild' wood. Owl aviaries.*

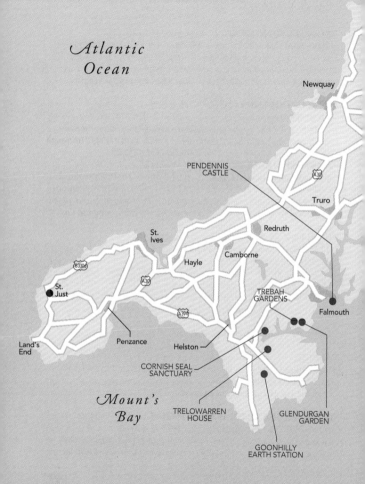

Atlantic
Ocean

Newquay

PENDENNIS
CASTLE

A30

Truro

St.
Ives

Redruth

B3306

Hayle

Camborne

St.
Just

A30

TREBAH
GARDENS

Land's
End

A394

Falmouth

Penzance

Helston

CORNISH SEAL
SANCTUARY

Mount's
Bay

TRELOWARREN
HOUSE

GLENDURGAN
GARDEN

GOONHILLY
EARTH STATION

PENDENNIS CASTLE (EH) Falmouth.
❑ 1000-1800 Easter-Sep.; 1000-1600 Tue.-Sun., Oct.-Easter.
❑ £1.60, concessions £1.20, child 5-16 80p.
A perfect example of the round type of coastal fort erected by Henry VIII in the 1540s. A recreation of a noisy gun-deck scene adds atmosphere.

TREBAH GARDENS 5 miles south of Falmouth.
❑ 1030-1700 (last entry). ❑ £1.80, child 5-15 80p.
A well-mapped route takes you down a long, steep valley garden of lawns, giant rhododendrons, pools, ferns, towering palms and 10-ft-high Brazilian rhubarb! Good, unobtrusive children's play area.

GLENDURGAN GARDEN (NT) 4.5 miles south of Falmouth.
❑ 1030-1730 Tue.-Sat., BH Mon., Mar.-Oct. ❑ £2, child 5-17 half price.
Similar in shape and style to Trebah (see above), Glendurgan is a 'plants-man's garden' with a fine maze, and culminates in the delightful tiny hamlet and small, sandy beach of Durgan.

CORNISH SEAL SANCTUARY Gweek.
❑ 0930-1800 summer. Feeding times 1100, 1600. ❑ £3.30, OAP £2.80, child £1.70.
The centrepiece of the sanctuary is the ten pools of lovable and lively seals revelling in their new homes in this beautiful riverside setting. Interpretation centre and walks.

TRELOWARREN HOUSE Mawgan.
❑ House 1430-1630 Wed., BH Mon., mid April-Oct.; also Sun. in high season. ❑ £1, child 50p. ❑ Craft shops 1100-1700 Easter-Sep.
The stables of this Tudor mansion are now a flourishing craft centre where potters and weavers can be seen at work. There is also a wood-land walk, a herb garden and an excellent bistro.

GOONHILLY EARTH STATION 7 miles south of Helston.
❑ 1000-1800 Easter-Oct. ❑ £2.50, OAP/child £1.50.
Millions of international telecommunications pass daily through the giant dish aerials here. Learn how in the tour and hands-on visitor centre.

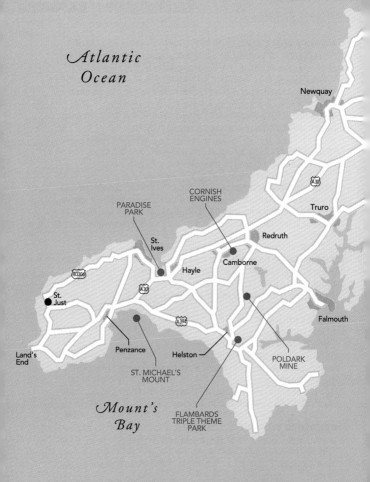

FLAMBARDS TRIPLE THEME PARK 3 miles southeast of Helston. ❏ 1000-1730 (last entry 1600) Easter-Oct. (closes 2030 late July-Aug.; last entry 1800). ❏ £6.99, OAP £3.50, child 4-13 £5.99. Reduced prices after 1430 (1600 late July-Aug.). Disabled.
The main attractions at this fine day out are the two fascinating recreations of a Victorian village and a street scene of Britain in the Blitz. There are also flight galleries, 24 aircraft, children's rides and an imaginative hands-on science discovery area.

POLDARK MINE Wendron, 3 miles north of Helston.
❏ 1000-1800 (last entry 1630) April-Oct. ❏ £3.75, OAP £3, child £2.25.
A fascinating insight into the lives of 19thC tin-miners is provided by a recreation of Winston Graham's 'Poldark' village and an unforgettable underground tour. Outstanding collection of mining machinery and artefacts. See **Mining**.

CORNISH ENGINES (NT) Pool, 2 miles west of Redruth.
❏ 1100-1800 April-Oct. (closes 1700 Oct.). ❏ £1.40, child 5-17 70p.
The most impressive working relics of the tin-mining industry, these giant engines were used for pumping up water from over 2000 ft below and for hauling up men and ore to the surface. See **Mining**.

PARADISE PARK Hayle.
❏ 1000-2000 May-early Sep., 1000-1800 early Sep.-April (last entry 2 hr before). ❏ £3.50, OAP £2.90, child £1.90.
Hundreds of colourful and exotic birds, including endangered parrots, flamingos and rare Cornish choughs, are displayed here in a beautiful, near-natural setting.

ST. MICHAEL'S MOUNT (NT) Marazion, 5 miles east of Penzance. ❏ 1030-1745 April-Oct.; tours as tide and weather allow, Nov.-Mar. ❏ £2.80, child 5-17 half price, family £7.50.
Parts of the enchanting small castle date back to the 17thC. Magnificent views and an excellent NT restaurant. See **A-Z**.

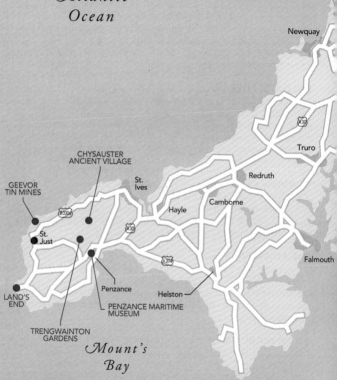

Atlantic Ocean

Newquay

A30

Truro

Redruth

CHYSAUSTER
ANCIENT VILLAGE

St. Ives

Hayle

Camborne

GEEVOR
TIN MINES

B3306

St.
Just

A30

Falmouth

LAND'S
END

Penzance

A394

PENZANCE MARITIME
MUSEUM

Helston

TRENGWAINTON
GARDENS

*Mount's
Bay*

PENZANCE MARITIME MUSEUM Chapel St, Penzance.
❑ 1000-1700 Mon.-Sat., Easter-mid Oct. ❑ £1, child 50p.
This colourful small museum takes the form of a four-storey 'between-deck' section of an early-18thC galleon. Cannon, model ships and figureheads conjure up a salty, nautical atmosphere.

TRENGWAINTON GARDENS (NT) 2 miles northwest of
Penzance. ❑ 1100-1800 Wed.-Sat., BH Mon., Good Fri., Mar.-Oct.
(closes 1700 Mar., Oct.) ❑ £1.80, child 5-17 half price.
One of the best collections of rare and subtropical plants and shrubs in the country. The gardens have a splendid view over Mount's Bay.

CHYSAUSTER ANCIENT VILLAGE (EH) 3.5 miles north of
Penzance. ❑ 1000-1800 Easter-Sep. ❑ 95p, OAP 75p, child 5-16 45p.
Eight sets of circular house walls and various other stones bear witness to the farming settlement which existed here c.100 BC-AD 250. The purpose of the underground tunnels ('fogous') is a mystery.

GEEVOR TIN MINES Pendeen.
❑ 1000-1700 Mon.-Fri., Easter-Oct. Underground tours at 1000, 1200,
1500. ❑ Tour £12.50, child 10-16 £10. Booking advisable; tel: 0736-788662. Small charge for museum.
Descend over 2000 ft into the old Levant mine, once one of Cornwall's most successful mines and, up until 1991, one of the last two mines still producing Cornish tin. A memorable experience. See **Mining***.*

LAND'S END
❑ Times and entrance charges vary by season; tel: 0736-871501.
❑ July-late Sep. (peak season) £4.50, OAP £2, child 5-14 £2.50.
Late entrance reductions.
This family entertainment complex features exhibitions on seafaring history, colourful Cornish characters, craft demonstrations and The Last Labyrinth, its multi-sensory historical-mythical tour de force with good special effects.

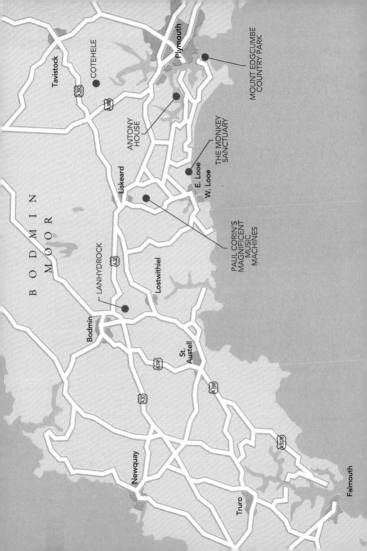

COTEHELE (NT) Near St. Dominick, 8 miles southwest of Tavistock.
❑ Grounds 1100-1800 April-Oct. (closes 1700 Oct.). House 1100-1800 Sat.-Thu., April-Oct. ❑ Grounds £2.20; plus house £4.40, child 5-17 half price. Disabled (partly).
This idyllically located house is the area's jewel in the crown. See **A-Z**.

MOUNT EDGCUMBE COUNTRY PARK Cremyll, Torpoint.
❑ Park 0800-dusk daily. ❑ Free. ❑ House & garden 1100-1730 Wed.-Sun. & BH Mon., Easter-Oct. ❑ £2.50, OAP £1.50, child under 16 £1.
Beautiful 18thC country park with formal gardens, deer park and magnificent sea views. The house, destroyed in 1941, is a Georgian replica.

ANTONY HOUSE (NT) 5 miles west of Plymouth, via Torpoint ferry.
❑ 1400-1800 Tue.-Thu., BH Mon., April-Oct.; also Sun. June-Aug.
❑ £3, child 5-17 half price.
Cornwall's best-preserved early-Georgian house boasts fine tapestries, a spacious library and Tudor and 18thC furniture.

PAUL CORIN'S MAGNIFICENT MUSIC MACHINES
St. Keyne Station, 3 miles south of Liskeard.
❑ 1100-1700 Easter-Oct. ❑ £2.50, child £1.25, family £7.50. Disabled.
Unique collection of carousel-organs, café-organs, street-organs, self-playing pianos and a 'Mighty Wurlitzer', all demonstrated by Paul Corin.

THE MONKEY SANCTUARY Murrayton, 4 miles east of Looe.
❑ 1030-1700 Sun.-Thu., Easter fortnight & May-Sep. ❑ £3, OAP £2, child £1.40. Disabled.
Unique conservation project set in beautiful grounds offers the chance to meet and touch engaging Amazonian Woolly Monkeys. Allow 2 hours.

LANHYDROCK (NT) 2.5 miles southeast of Bodmin.
❑ Garden 1100-1800 April-Oct. (1700 Oct.); dawn-dusk Nov.-Mar. House 1100-1800 Tue.-Sun., BH Mon., April-Oct. (1700 Oct). ❑ Garden £2.40; plus house £4.20, child 5-17 half price. Disabled (partly).
Interior of this spacious 17thC house was mostly rebuilt in the 1880s but notable parts have been retained. Famous for its gardens and river walks.

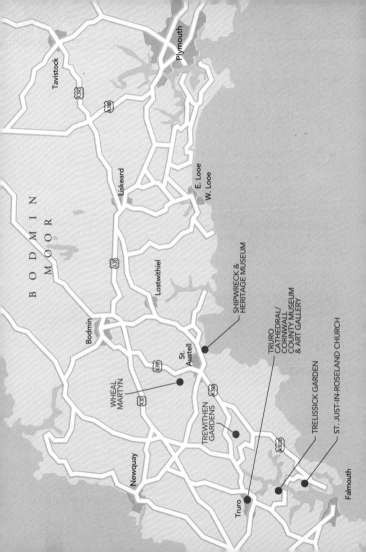

WHEAL MARTYN (China Clay Museum) Carthew.
❑ 1000-1800 (last entry 1700) Easter-Oct. ❑ £3.50, child £1.75.
An interesting and lucid outdoor historic trail takes you by the old
machinery and explains the methods of producing china clay. Adjacent
is a nature trail and a spectacular view into a working pit. See **Mining**.

SHIPWRECK & HERITAGE MUSEUM Charlestown.
❑ 1000-1600 (later in high season) April-Oct. ❑ £2, OAP £1.50, child
£1, family £5.
Britain's largest collection of shipwreck artefacts plus china-clay exhibits
are displayed in the tunnels of an old clay-drying area (see **Mining***).*

TREWITHEN GARDENS Probus.
❑ Garden 1000-1630 Mon.-Sat., Mar.-Sep. House 1400-1630 Mon.,
Tue., April-July. ❑ Garden £1.50, child 50p; plus house £2.75.
See the introductory video before touring the splendid 20-acre gardens
of camellias, rhododendrons, rare trees and shrubs.

TRURO CATHEDRAL Truro.
Built 1880-1910 in grand and spacious 13thC style, the great central
tower rises 250 ft and stands cheek-by-jowl with its modern neighbours.

CORNWALL COUNTY MUSEUM & ART GALLERY Truro.
❑ 0900-1700 Mon.-Sat. ❑ 50p, OAP 25p, child free.
This lively collection includes maritime history, natural history, china
clay (see **Mining***), English porcelain, pewter, glass and the Opie Gallery.*

TRELISSICK GARDEN (NT) 4 miles south of Truro.
❑ 1100-1800 Mon.-Sat., 1300-1800 Sun., Mar.-Oct. (closes 1700 Mar.,
Oct.). ❑ £2.50, child 5-17 half price. Disabled.
A garden of rhododendrons, exotic trees, etc. in a magnificent setting
overlooking the Fal estuary. Fine craft gallery; lovely barn restaurant.

ST. JUST-IN-ROSELAND CHURCH St. Just-in-Roseland.
A garden of subtropical plants and ancient gravestones tumbles down to
a tiny church by a wooded creek. An English idyll; go when the tide is in.

Ilfracombe harbour

Accommodation: In high season you should try to book well in advance but if you turn up with nowhere to stay, the nearest tourist information centre will help you (there is a small booking fee). Bed and breakfasts (B&B), boarding houses and guesthouses are the cheapest lodgings aside from camping and youth hostels. The *West Country B&B Touring Map* recommends over 130 establishments for £16 or less per person per night (based on twin occupancy). All establishments listed by the tourist board conform to minimum standards and range from 'listed' (clean and comfortable but with few facilities) to the top-of-the-range five crowns with the most comprehensive facilities and service. Expect to pay £25-35 (more if over two crowns) per couple per night. A full list can be found in *West Country Where to Stay* (£2.50), available from the West Country Tourist Board. In addition to the tourist board's crown system, the AA and RAC also rank hotels on a one- to five-star rating. Expect to pay the following per couple per night for a double room: two stars £40-75, three/four stars £60-90. See **Camping & Caravanning**, **Tourist Information**, **Youth Hostels**.

Appledore: 3 miles north of Bideford. Pop: 2200. The centre of Charles Kingsley's 'little white fishing village' has changed little in two centuries and many of the tiny terraced cottages in the tight network of narrow, cobbled streets date from the 18thC. The atmosphere is peaceful and almost Mediterranean, with several brightly painted houses. Explore along Market St and Bude St and you will come to the North Devon Maritime Museum, a wholly appropriate setting for a fine collection depicting the development of shipbuilding, a trade still carried on in Appledore today (1100-1300, 1400-1730 Mon.-Fri., Easter-Oct. 80p, OAP 50p, child 5-16 20p).

Barnstaple: Pop: 19,200. The most important and most interesting town in north Devon. Much of Barnstaple's compact centre has been sympathetically modernized, and it harmonizes well with the old town. Pick up a map of guided walks from the tourist information centre and make sure you see the following: St. Anne's Chapel and Old Grammar School, built in 1330 (1000-1300, 1400-1630 Mon.-Sat. exc. Wed. pm, June-Oct. Free); the 17thC Church Lane almshouses (not open to the public) and adjacent Old School Coffee House – an excellent refreshment stop; and the Museum of North Devon, a fine collection of local history, natural science and art (1000-1630 Tue.-Sat. Free). This is also the best place from which to view Barnstaple's famous medieval 16-arch Long Bridge.

Barnstaple offers the best shopping in the area, and continues its tradition as a regional-produce centre in its pannier markets (see **A-Z**), held in the 19thC iron-and-glass-roofed market hall (0800-1600 Tue., Fri., Sat.). Alongside is Butcher's Row, an epicurean terrace of traditional butchers, fishmongers and delicatessens in small, stable-like premises. The pannier market hosts a craft fair (1000-1600 Thu., May-Sep., & Mon., July-Sep.) and an antique market (1000-1500 Wed.). Brannam's Pottery is a noted local industry. The original works at Litchdon Lane (off the riverside road) retains a curious old shop selling seconds and end-of-line bargains; the new works, where you can take a guided tour, is a mile out of town (1000-1700 Mon.-Sat.; also Sun., July-Aug. £1.50, OAP £1.25, child 5-16 75p, family £4). There is a cattle market every Fri., and the annual town fair is held on the Wed. before 20 Sep.

Beaches: Devon and Cornwall have some of the best and cleanest beaches in Britain, regularly taking 14-15 Blue Flags out of a total of around 30 awarded annually to the whole of Britain. The European Blue Flag award is given on the basis of water quality, standards of safety and visitor facilities, and those beaches which have received the award in the last 3 years are listed in the **BEACHES** pages (by county). Given that Cornwall alone has over 300 public beaches, these lists are only a small selection, chosen largely on the basis of facilities, cleanliness and accessibility (both in terms of proximity to popular resorts and ease of immediate access). Beaches off the beaten track are included, however, and often the closest beaches to a resort centre have been excluded, as these are mentioned in the town's resort review in the A-Z. In Cornwall, a 'porth' beach is a cove (typically at the mouth of a valley) and 'towans' are sand dunes. As a general rule, you will find Atlantic rollers on the north- and west-facing coasts (great for surfing) whereas south coasts are more mellow. All beaches in the **BEACHES** pages have lifeguards throughout the summer. Pay heed to warning flags and never swim near a river estuary as it meets the sea. You can expect a 5- or 10-min walk to many beaches and a car-parking charge. For more comprehensive coverage, buy *The West Country Beach Guide* or *Popular & Secluded Beaches of Cornwall*. See **DEVON-BEACHES, CORNWALL-BEACHES**.

Beer: 9 miles east of Sidmouth. Pop: 1300. A fishing village famous for its picture-postcard pebble beach strewn with serried ranks of colourful fishing craft. It is also renowned locally for Beer quarry stone which often appears in the same postcard in the form of the huge, white, backing cliffs. You can take a 60-min tour of the quarry caves and museum (1000-1800 Easter-Sep., 1100-1600 Oct. £2.20, OAP/child 5-16 £1.55) and visit Beer Pecorama, a pleasure garden with a miniature railway and children's entertainments (1000-1730 Mon.-Fri., 1000-1300 Sat., Sun., Easter, late May-Aug. £2.15 summer, £1.70 spring, child 85p).

Berrynarbor: 4 miles east of Ilfracombe. Pop: 750. This outstanding unspoiled village lies in a deep, protected valley and is dominated by its splendid 96-ft-tall, 15thC church tower. Ye Olde Globe Inn, some 200 years younger (though housed in 13thC cottages) is well worth a visit. Around the pub are equally ancient cottages, pretty tearooms and timbered and thatched houses. A mile away is the picturesque, peaceful Watermouth Bay and Watermouth Castle. This imposing medieval-looking fortress, actually built in 1825, houses an imaginative Disney-style amusement park which will delight kids and amuse their parents (see **DEVON-EXCURSION 3, DEVON-WHAT TO SEE 1**). Allow 3 hours for a visit here.

Bickleigh: 9 miles north of Exeter. Pop: 200. The two halves of this pretty village on the River Exe are connected by a 300-year-old bridge. Whitewashed cottages and the church perch on the hill above, Bickleigh Mill is below, and to the other side of the bridge the picturesque Trout Inn and more thatched cottages slope down to an idyllic riverbank scene. Bickleigh Castle (see **DEVON-WHAT TO SEE 6**) also lies on this side.

Bicycle & Motorcycle Hire: The abundance of steep hills in Devon and Cornwall, many with 1-in-5 gradients, is a major deterrent to once-a-year cyclists. However, bicycle hire is available at many large centres. Sample prices are £8 per day for a 12-speed bike, and £5 per day or £25 per week for a mountain bike. Ask at the tourist information centre for details on local cycle trails. Three recommended easy scenic rides are the Plym Valley, from Lara Bridge, Plymouth, to Goodameavy on the edge of Dartmoor; the Camel Trail, which follows the Camel Estuary from Padstow to beyond Bodmin via Wadebridge; and the North Devon Coastal Cycleway around the Taw and Torridge Estuary (hire points at Braunton, Barnstaple and Instow). Motorcycle and moped hire is much less common. In west Cornwall, try Blewett & Pender, Albert St, Penzance (moped £10 per day, inc. insurance and crash helmet).

Bideford: 9 miles southwest of Barnstaple. Pop: 12,300. Like Barnstaple (see **A-Z**), Bideford boasts a famous medieval Long Bridge and a traditional pannier market (Tue., Sat.; see **A-Z**). In Elizabethan times it grew in prosperity and for a time was England's largest provincial port. The Broad Quay, from where Lundy (see **A-Z**) sailings depart, and some surviving merchants' houses in Bridgeland St, are reminders of those heady days. Shopping facilities are good, with several antique shops on High St and an open-air market (1000-1600 Wed.). The Burton Art Gallery holds an interesting collection of paintings, pottery, pewter and splendid visiting-card cases (1000-1300, 1400-1700 Mon.-Sat., 1400-1700 Sun., April-Sep.; closed Mon. pm & Sun., Oct.-Mar. Free). Two miles away at Instow is Tapeley Park, a smallish William & Mary house (late 17thC), with Morris furniture and Italianate gardens. The main attraction here, though, is jousting (house tours by demand; min. 15 people. £1.50, child £1. Gardens 1000-1800 Easter-Oct. £2, OAP £1.50, child £1. Jousting 1400/1430 Sun., Wed., Fri. £3.50, OAP £2.80, child £2; inc. entry to gardens).

Boat Trips: Nearly every seaside town, port or even estuary village will offer you the chance to take to the water. The following trips are particularly worthwhile: River Fal, River Helford and creek cruises from Falmouth; dockyards, warships and points of historic interest in Plymouth Sound; River Dart cruises from Dartmouth, Totnes or Torbay, with the round trip from Paignton to Kingswear travelling by steam train (30 min), ferry to Dartmouth (10 min), cruise to Totnes (90 min) and a 20-min return by bus to Paignton being highly recommended (£7, child £5).

If you are in a group and would like to charter a vessel privately, professionally crewed yachts capable of taking a party of 12 are available for hire in Torquay and other popular ports at around £300 per day (for Torquay, tel: 0803-215166). See **Lundy**, **Water Sports**.

Bodmin: 19 miles east of Newquay. Pop: 12,250. Much of the character of this former county town unfortunately has been swept away by modernization, although there are still some points of interest scattered around. In the centre stands its mighty 15thC church and Tudor Guildhall, and nearby is the once-notorious Bodmin Jail where some of its grim past is recreated (1000-1800 Sun.-Fri., Easter-mid Oct. £2.50, child £1.25). Just to the east of the centre is Bodmin Steam Railway which runs a short scenic service, and 2 miles further on at Fletchers Bridge lies Bodmin Farm Park (1000-1800 Sun.-Fri., mid May-Sep. £2, OAP £1.50, child £1). Three miles north is Pencarrow House, a handsome Georgian mansion with a good paintings collection (1330-1700 Sun.-Thu., Easter-mid Oct. £2.50, OAP £1.20, child £1. Gardens only 50p).

Bodmin Moor: With an area of c.150 sq. miles this is the smallest and least elevated of the three major West Country moors. At its heart, at Bolventor, stands Jamaica Inn, the old smuggler's inn immortalized by Daphne Du Maurier (now highly commercialized). Just north of here is Brown Willy, at 1377 ft the moor's highest peak. Aside from the major centres of Liskeard and Launceston (see **A-Z**), there are several interesting settlements on Bodmin Moor. St. Neot, lying in an attractive wooded valley, is probably the pick of these. The splendid 15thC church is famous for its rare medieval glass, and The London, next door, is a fine village local. Six miles east lies The Cheesewring, a huge and bizarre, though naturally formed, pile of disc-shaped stones. A circle of standing stones known as The Hurlers and the Trethevy Quoit are also close by. The latter is the most dramatic of all Cornwall's neolithic remains, standing 8-10 ft high and comprising a number of upright stone slabs topped by a horizontal capstone. It functioned as a burial chamber and was once covered by a 130-ft-long earth mound. St. Cleer, nearby, is worth a visit as are Altarnun, Blisland and Cardinham.

Boscastle: 3 miles northeast of Tintagel. Pop: 750. Boscastle is famed for its much-photographed tiny harbour which nestles in a narrow cleft of the jagged-slate cliffs so typical of this area. The approach to the breakwater is by way of a babbling, crystal-clear stream lined with ancient slate-and-quarrystone houses and tearooms. Among these is the Museum of Witchcraft which documents magic in the West Country in an entertaining and explicit exhibition (1000-1730 Easter-late June, early Sep.-mid Oct.; 1000-2100 late June-early Sep. £1, OAP/child 10-16 60p, under 10s 40p). Boscastle's other attractions include the Cave, an exhibition of illusions featuring 3-D photography and holograms (1000-1800 April-late July, Sep., Oct.; 1000-2100 late July-Aug. £1.25,

OAP/student £1, child 5-16 75p, family £3), and two good pubs, The Napoleon and The Wellington. See **CORNWALL-EXCURSION**.

Braunton: 9 miles south of Woolacombe. Pop: 8000. Behind the modern main-street facade lies a pleasant old village with a lovely 13thC church and, at Hillsview, the Elliot Gallery, north Devon's largest display of paintings and craftwork (1000-1700 Easter-Oct.; 1030-1630 Tue.-Sat., Oct.-Easter. 50p, child free). The adjacent Braunton Burrows is a totally natural grass-and-dune coastal plain, ending at Saunton Sands. It is a mecca for naturalists.

Brixham: 8 miles south of Torquay. Pop: 11,900. Brixham's compact, picturesque harbour is a very different side of Torbay to the over-commercialized seafront sprawl of its neighbours, and the blend of old and new is altogether much more harmonious here. On the harbour front, climb aboard the replica of the *Golden Hind* to see the conditions under which local hero Sir Francis Drake circumnavigated the globe in the 16thC (0900-2100 Easter-mid Oct. £1, child 60p). You would do well to avoid the adjacent Perils of the Deep exhibition and instead, see the local aquarium (1000-2200 Mar.-Oct. 75p, child 50p) and the interesting local museum (1000-1730 Mon.-Sat. £1, OAP/child 50p, family £2.50). Take a look at the busy working marina near the harbour, and don't miss the unspoiled beauty of Berry Head.

Bude: 31 miles southwest of Barnstaple. Pop: 5660. This popular Victorian resort has a very different look from most of its coastal neighbours as it doesn't face the sea. Instead, it is built around a valley through which the River Neet and the 19thC Bude Canal flow. Once described as 'the least rowdy resort in the country', Bude still exudes a quiet atmosphere and on sunny days most activity is confined to its fine beaches (see **CORNWALL-BEACHES 1**). In less clement weather a walk out onto the breakwater beside the canal gives an invigorating view across the wild coastline. By the canal is a small folk museum (1100-1600 April-Oct. 50p, OAP/child 25p) and the Lower Wharf Gallery & Craft Shop. Bude comes alive in the last eight days of Aug. when New Orleans comes to Cornwall in the shape of a top-quality jazz festival.

Budleigh Salterton: 13 miles southeast of Exeter. Pop: 4500. This genteel resort has a lovely Blue Flag pebble beach (see **DEVON-BEACHES 2**) overlooked by splendid cliff-top walks (get a leaflet on these from the tourist information centre). Visit the Fairlynch Museum (1330-1630 Mon.-Sat., Easter-mid July, Sep., Oct.; 1030-1630 mid July-Aug. 60p, OAP/child 30p), a lovely thatched house with local-history, craft and costume exhibits. Artist Sir John Millais put the town on the map by painting *The Boyhood of Raleigh* here. Raleigh was born 2 miles north at Hayes Barton in a farmhouse which is now a guesthouse. Nearby is the pretty village of East Budleigh.

Burgh Island: 5 miles west of Kingsbridge. You can walk across from Bigbury-on-Sea to this 28-acre island at low tide, and there are at least three good reasons for going. The first is the Pilchard Inn, housed in the last remaining cottage of a once-thriving fishing community dating back to the 14thC. Rather more opulent is the splendid Art Deco Burgh Island Hotel, now restored to its former glory as in the days when it was the haunt of Noël Coward, the Duke of Windsor and Mrs Simpson, and Agatha Christie (who set *Evil Under The Sun* here), among others. If you want to see inside you will have to book a meal or cream tea (tel: 0548-810514). The third attraction is your means of return, an extraordinary sea-tractor which has a passenger compartment high above its wheels and can make the island crossing safely in up to 7 ft of water!

Camping & Caravanning: There are good facilities for caravanning and camping all over this area. Prices vary considerably, but start at £130 per caravan per week in high season (average £180-200) and £60 in low season (average £100). Prices per tent per night range from £5-7. See *West Country Holiday Parks* (free from tourist information centres), *FHG Guide to Caravan & Camping Holidays, Caravans & Chalet Park Guide, Where to Stay Camping & Caravan Parks*, or ask at the nearest tourist information centre.

Children: The vast majority of tourism in the West Country caters for families and even on a rainy day you will have no difficulty in keeping children busy. To save money look for family attractions with all-inclusive ticket prices and remember you can take a picnic to most outdoor attractions. In the evenings there are 'family pubs' in most resorts and many hotels offer child-minding services.

Chudleigh: 9 miles north of Torquay. Pop: 1250. This small market centre has several attractions in its vicinity. The Wheel Craft Centre in the town includes craftsmen at work, a mill tour and a good restaurant (tour 1000-1730. £1, OAP/child 50p). Two miles away on the A 38 is Silverlands, a family-entertainment centre with a mix of exhibitions and live entertainments (1000-1800. £3, OAP £2.50, child 4-14 £1.75).

Clovelly: 16 miles north of Bude. Pop: 420. This impossibly pretty fishing village is the West Country's favourite 'pin-up'. Take the scenic approach along Hobby Drive to the car park perched high above the town. From here on cars are banned and there is an admission fee of £1 to the village, which is privately owned. Stop at the visitor centre and see the video before descending the precipitous half-mile cobbled lane to the waterfront. Landrovers and donkeys cater for the aged, infirm or simply tired, at 50p per ride. Commendably, Clovelly heavily restricts the amount of tourism development so you will see no fish-and-chip shops or tawdry souvenir stalls. There are very few holiday cottages and only two pub/hotels. If you go late or very early to avoid the crowds you will find the atmosphere in the narrow, floral-decked, whitewashed alleyways timeless, serene and very Mediterranean.

Clovelly

Combe Martin: 6 miles east of Ilfracombe. Pop: 2300. Nominally a village, Combe Martin has a main street which straggles along for nearly 2 miles, ending at a pleasant beach-harbour flanked by green hills. On High St stands the eccentrically built Pack of Cards Inn, designed to resemble a house of playing cards, a fine 15thC church and, close to the harbour, the Combe Martin Motorcycle Collection, featuring 20-30 antique British bikes (1000-1800 late May-mid Sep. £1, OAP/child 7+ 50p). Outside the village on the A 399 is Combe Martin Wildlife Park and, 2 miles south at Berry Down, Farm World features domestic and agricultural bygones, farm animals and craft demonstrations (1030-1830 Easter-Oct. £2.80, child £1.40). See **DEVON-EXCURSION 3**.

Cornish Language: Until it officially died out in 1777, Cornwall's residents had their own Celtic language, and recently there has been a resurgence of interest in the ancient tongue. This is most manifest in the annual Gorsedd, or Meeting, of the Bards of Kernow, when awards are made to prominent Cornish songwriters and poets (see **Events**).
The following are common Cornish place names, suffixes and prefixes:

Carn – rock pile	Pol – pool/pond
Chy – house	Porth – cove
Goon – down	Towan – sandhill/dune
Kernow – Cornwall	Tre – homestead/hamlet
Pen – chief/hill/headland	Wheal – (mine) workings

Cotehele: Near St. Dominick. This outstanding house has been occupied only occasionally, and is therefore little altered, since medieval times. Glowing tapestries, ancient furnishings, pewter and armour adorn atmospheric rooms which have never seen artificial light. A walk through the gardens brings you to Cotehele Quay on the Tamar. The setting is a 19thC rural idyll. Alongside the peaceful, grassy riverbank is moored the *Shamrock*, the last surviving Tamar sailing barge. The old Edgcumbe Arms is now a delightful tearoom and restaurant, and there is also a small maritime museum. A woodland walk leads to the manor water mill which houses craft workings. See **CORNWALL-WHAT TO SEE 5**.

Croyde: 5 miles south of Woolacombe. Pop: (inc. Mortehoe) 1446. This small, attractive roadside village is famous for its bay and popular beach (see **DEVON-BEACHES 1**). A local-craft centre, a good pub and the Croyde Rock & Gem Museum (1000-1700 Mar.-June, Sep., Oct.; 1000-2200 July-Aug.; tel: 0271-8904047 for entry charges) are wet-weather alternatives. Baggy Point, beyond the bay, offers fine coastal views.

Dartington: 2 miles north of Totnes. Dartington is the home of a fascinating 60-year-old project in rural regeneration which has established a small community involved in education, research, business and the arts. Their most conspicuous achievement is Dartington Crystal, at Great Torrington (see **DEVON-WHAT TO SEE 1**). Although the house is not really a tourist attraction, its hall and garden are open to visitors when not in use (Free; donation requested). The Cider Press Centre is a shopping and eating attraction and includes fine crafts, glass, toys and speciality foods plus a branch of Cranks vegetarian restaurant (0930-1730 daily, summer; Mon.-Sat. winter).

Dartmoor: At 365 sq. miles, Dartmoor is the largest of the three main moorlands in the region and, like Exmoor, has been a national park since 1951. In geological make-up, however, the two are quite different: Dartmoor's bracken- and heather-covered uplands are interrupted by its distinctive granite outcrops which rear up so starkly, often along fault lines in the ground. There is a long history of habitation on the moor, with evidence indicating settlement dating back at least 6000 years, as well as an impressive array of prehistoric remains in the form of stone circles and burial chambers. Settlement today is much less stark and more picturesque, with showcase villages like Buckland-in-the-Moor and Widecombe-in-the-Moor (see **A-Z**) inevitably attracting hundreds of day-trippers in summer. The best way to appreciate the area's diversity, however, and to get away from the madding crowd, is to get out and walk. There is a full programme of guided and do-it-yourself walks available from National Park offices and tourist information centres (see **Walking**); get a copy of the *Dartmoor Visitor* for details. See **DEVON-EXCURSION 1, DEVON-WALKS**.

Dartmouth: 10 miles south of Torquay (by ferry). Pop: 6200. This ancient town enjoys a marvellous situation at the mouth of the River Dart, with steep hills providing a picturesque backdrop to the busy, colourful boating estuary. Winding, cobbled streets and narrow alleyways full of antique shops and well-preserved houses crisscross the old town (free maps at the tourist information centre). Don't miss Bayard's Cove, a short, cobbled quay lined with 18thC houses; the Butterwalk, a terrace of 17thC shops and a local museum (1100-1700 Mon.-Sat. 60p, child 20p);

the old shambles area of Fairfax Quay; and the atmospheric 14thC Cherub pub. There is also a fine church and the old pannier market (see **A–Z**), now occupied by craftspeople; another local museum on Anzac St; and the Newcomen Engine House. The main attraction, however, is Dartmouth Castle (EH 1000-1800 Easter-Sep., 1000-1600 Oct.-Easter. £1.30, OAP 95p, child 5-16 65p), a short boat trip away. A trip up the Dart, one of Britain's most scenic waters, is also recommended.

Dawlish: 11 miles north of Torquay. Pop: 11,000. The most famous feature of this old-fashioned resort is The Lawn, a landscaped strip of garden flanked by two streams which are home to black and white swans. There are a few fine Regency buildings but the centre has been over-commercialized and has little else of interest apart from the local museum (1000-1230, 1400-1700 Mon.-Sat., 1400-1700 Sun., May-Sep. 50p, child 25p). The beach is not a peaceful retreat, as mainline trains thunder past just feet away! Dawlish Warren is a far better alternative.

Disabled People: The term 'Disabled' in the attractions listed in the blue section of this book is intended to indicate those places which we recommend that wheelchair users visit. It does not imply international access standards. In some cases only parts of the attractions are accessible; this is indicated by 'Disabled (partly)'. There are several detailed sources of information for wheelchair tourists in Devon and Cornwall, including national guides. Among the latter are *Holidays in the British Isles – A Guide for Disabled People* by RADAR and *Guide for the Disabled Traveller* by the AA. Other good references are the National Trust's booklet *Information for Visitors with Disabilities* and the West Country Tourist Board's *Places to Visit* which uses the internationally approved wheelchair symbol. There is also a national holiday-care service, tel: 0293-774535. Telephone the following numbers for information on Devon: Honiton, tel: 0404-41212; Plymouth, tel: 0752-665084; Exeter, tel: 0392-64205. There is also the Holiday Services company, tel: 0626-779424. Access guides include the *Devon Holiday Accommodation Guide for Disabled People*, available from the tourist board, and *Dartmoor for the Disabled* (send an SAE to the Dartmoor National Park Authority, Parke, Bovey Tracey).
In Cornwall, Personal Mobility of Probus (near Truro) run a special transport service, tel: 0726-883460, and Churchtown Field Studies Centre at Lanlivery runs excellent outward-bound courses.

Discos: The most popular nightspots are in Torquay and Newquay. Torquay has eight clubs, ranging from Monroe's and The Hideaway, catering for the younger market, to the swanky Mariner's at the Imperial Hotel, which aims at a 'more discerning' crowd. Newquay's top club is the Tall Trees at the Blue Lagoon Leisure Centre. Other popular resort club/discos include The Cornwall Coliseum near St. Austell, the Inn on The Park at Paignton and Scandal's and Peggoty's at St. Ives. Resort discos are usually cheap and cheerful, with a cover charge of £2-4 and drinks prices 50% above pub equivalents, but they are often offset by 'special nights' sponsored by drinks companies. Penzance boasts the classy Zero-Berkeley with an Egon Ronay-recommended restaurant, the new dockside development at Exeter has two nightspots, and Ritzy's and The Academy are the places to be seen in Plymouth.

Drewsteignton: 13 miles west of Exeter. Pop: 1250. A picturesque cob and thatched village, around a central square, standing high above lush, heavily wooded Teign Gorge. After a drink at the wonderfully old-fashioned Drewe Arms take a walk down to the local beauty spot of Fingle Bridge, carrying on to Castle Drogo (see **DEVON-WHAT TO SEE 4**).

Driving: The fastest way to Devon and Cornwall is on the M 4 and M 5 then via the A 30 or A 38, both of which have long sections of dual carriageway. The A 361 is north Devon's main artery, while the A 39 is recommended for its scenery but not its speed. Driving on the minor roads can be difficult, with 1-in-5 gradients commonplace and lanes so narrow as barely to accommodate one car, let alone two abreast. Be patient, be prepared to stop and reverse and at the height of the season expect lengthy queues into most towns and popular villages. Use either park-and-ride services or the large car parks on the outskirts of towns.

Eating Out: The general standard of eating out in this part of the world has been debased for years in order to cater for the low-budget tourist. Standards have improved recently but the number of good restaurants and standard of pub catering is still depressingly low. Aside from the establishments listed (by county) in **RESTAURANTS**, your best bet is probably the fish-and-chip shop. For lunch and tea, National Trust restaurants are slightly expensive but always produce good-quality food, usually in pleasant surroundings. 'Meadery' restaurants are common in south Cornwall, taking the 'Olde English' theme of mead (or blackberry wine) and 'chicken in the rough' (eaten with your fingers) served in bierkeller-style halls – good fun if you're with a group. See **Food & Drink**.

Events: *30 April/1 May:* 'Obby 'Oss Celebrations, Padstow (see **Padstow**); *8 May:* Helston Furry Dance (see **Helston**); *mid May:* Devon County Show, Westpoint, Exeter.

1st weekend in June: Royal Cornwall Show, Wadebridge; Truro Festival of Song & Dance, various venues in Truro and Falmouth; *mid-late June:* Sidmouth International Folk Arts Festival (see **Sidmouth**); Exeter Festival; *mid June:* Brixham Folk, Song & Dance Festival.

2nd-3rd week in July: Torbay Carnival; *3rd week:* Exmouth Carnival Week; *late July:* International Air Day, Culdrose near Helston.

Mid August: Heavy Horse Show, Tregony, near Truro; *last week in August:* Torbay Royal Regatta.

First Saturday in September: Gorsedd of the Bards of Kernow (see **Cornish Language**); *Second Tuesday:* Widecombe Fair.

Exeter: Pop: 97,000. The two principal areas of tourist interest in this thriving university town are the cathedral and the quay. In the shadow of the famous Norman and medieval structure, Cathedral Close is a charming, peaceful row of shops and houses, some dating back to the 15thC. Both Mol's Coffee House (1596),

now a silver and goldsmith's shop, and the popular Ship Inn in St. Martin's Lane, claim patronage by Sir Francis Drake. Parallel to the Close runs High St which, though mutilated by modern development, still retains some fine half-timbered buildings, including the 14thC Guildhall (1000-1700 Mon.-Sat. Free). Further along is Gandy St, quiet, cobbled and unspoiled with good eating options. Just off High St are the Underground Passages where you can walk through the medieval tunnels which originally carried water to Exeter (1400-1700 Tue.-Sat. £1, OAP/child 50p). Go on to the Royal Albert Memorial Museum & Art Gallery and the Priory of St. Nicholas, off Fore St (1000-1300, 1400-1730 Tue.-Sat.). En route to the quay, drop in at the rambling, atmospheric White Hart, and almost opposite is the excellent Global Village ethnic-crafts shop and garden-café. The quay itself is in the early stages of being trendified, with antiques and craft shops and eating, drinking and nightspots. The Quay Interpretation Centre (1000-1700 Sep.-June, 1000-1800 July, Aug. Closed 1300-1400 Sat., Sun. & BH. Free) is the perfect introduction before visiting the Maritime Museum. This outstanding collection of exotic craft (in the setting used for filming parts of *The Onedin Line*) alone is worth the trip to Exeter. Several interesting walking tours are also on offer, and many are free. Details can be had from the tourist information centre at the Civic Centre, off Southernhay. See **DEVON-WHAT TO SEE 5**, **Events**.

Exmoor: Like Dartmoor, Exmoor is a national park governed by strict conservation laws. Most of its 265 sq. miles lie in Somerset but the northwest Devon corner, stretching west to Combe Martin, is as spectacular and varied as anywhere. Sparse upland ridges covered in bracken and heather give way to rolling, verdant pastures, and streams and ravines meet in spectacular beauty spots. Just inside the Devon border is Doone Valley, immortalized by R. D. Blackmore in his novel *Lorna Doone* (1869). Ponies, red deer, Devon Red cattle and Exmoor Horn and Devon Closewool sheep wander freely over the moor. Pick up a copy of the *Exmoor Visitor* at a tourist information centre, for details of events and guided walks. See **DEVON-EXCURSION 3**, **DEVON-WALKS**.

Exmouth: 11 miles south of Exeter. Pop: 29,000. This long-established resort enjoys a pleasant setting where the sea meets the Exe, with green, rolling hills beyond. The beach is good (see **DEVON-BEACHES 2**) and the town is clean and well-kept, catering for the good, old-fashioned, British-seaside holiday-maker. The world's largest 00-gauge model railway (1030-1730. £1.25, concessions 90p, child 5+ 70p) and the local museum (1000-1230, 1430-1630 Mon.-Fri.; 1000-1230 Sat., April-Oct. Free) are the town's only attractions but there are several river and sea trips. Nearby is the fascinating À La Ronde (see **DEVON-WHAT TO SEE 5**) and The World of Country Life at Sandy Bay. This re-creation of rural Devon's past features agricultural bygones, vintage cars and steam engines (1000-1700 Easter-Oct. £2.75, OAP/child £1.65). Exmouth Carnival Week is the third week in July.

Falmouth: Pop: 18,300. Once the busiest provincial port in England, Falmouth is now one of Cornwall's principal holiday resorts. For the most part, however, it has steered clear of burger bars and amusement arcades and has retained much of its old maritime atmosphere. Nowhere is this more the case than at the Custom House Quay where you will find the porticoed white Custom House (1814) and the *St. Denys* steam tug, the floating part of Falmouth's maritime museum (1000-1600 April-Oct./Nov. 65p, child 5-14 40p). Note also the 'King's Pipe' chimney stack where contraband tobacco used to be burned. The other half of the small maritime collection (1000-1600. 75p, child 45p, family £2.20) is back towards the Pleasure Boat Pier. A boat trip along the River Fal from here is highly recommended. The delightful Georgian De Wynn's Coffee House is the most attractive of the town's many refreshment stops. Just out of town the docks still thrive and, as you pass the once-vital fortification of Pendennis Castle (see **CORNWALL-WHAT TO SEE 2**) and head around the small peninsula you will find Falmouth's fine beaches and promenade (see **CORNWALL-BEACHES 4**).

Food & Drink: Although the renaissance of interest in locally produced foods is as strong in the West Country as anywhere, you will have to search to find it. You probably won't find it on the guesthouse menu but you could start the day with real-meat sausages, ham or bacon (the best come from Heal's Farm near South Molton), followed by a slice of saffron bread or a bun for elevenses, then the ubiquitous pasty for lunch. The best pasties should include chunks of skirt beef but most only have a desultory smattering of dubious-quality mince. Try the pasties made by Warrens, a chain of Cornish bakeries. Wash this down with scrumpy, the vernacular for locally produced cider (several places demonstrate the art of cider-making). Afternoon tea generally comprises scones and clotted cream, but for a change try Cornish Splits – small, soft, white-bread buns. Although local fish usually appears on the menu, don't expect too great a variety or a particularly cheap price. Look out for pollack, megrim, gurnard and local river trout. For smoked fish, try Salcombe Smokers at Kingsbridge, and for oysters, visit the Duchy of Cornwall's Oyster Farm at Port Navas, near Falmouth. Similarly, local wines are not common in restaurants but there are several vineyards you can tour, the best known being at Loddiswell, near Kingsbridge. Local cheeses are also fashionable; the best outlet is probably Ticklemore's in Totnes. See **Eating Out**.

Fowey: (pronounced 'Foy') 10 miles west of Looe (by ferry). Pop: 2150. The roofscape and river views of this lovely, unspoiled, historic town are unforgettable. Parking is extremely limited so you will have to leave your car at the top of the hill on which the town sits and make the steep descent to Fore St. Turn left past the Ship Inn, built in 1570, and visit the splendid 17thC church. Next to it is 'Place' – a towering, castellated, 14thC mansion best seen from above (not open to public). Back in Fore St, Noah's Ark, now a craft shop, dates from 1457 and retains some of its original kitchen. There are several more arts and crafts outlets around the town. Visit the local museum, which used to house the town clink, and for more history take a guided walk (1100 Tue., late May-Sep. £1.50, child 50p. Depart from the Quay). The only disappointment in this charming town is its lack of a good pub. Try the Safe Harbour, uphill from the Quay, or better still take the ferry over to either Bodinnick or picturesque Polruan where good hostelries can be found. Polruan also boasts the fine, sandy cove of Lantic Bay.

Hartland: 15 miles north of Bude. Pop: 1400. This is the remotest corner of Devon and when the wind blows, undoubtedly its wildest. From Hartland Quay to the Point is a feared ships' graveyard but on a quiet day it possesses a savage beauty. Two miles west of the town is Stoke, famous for its splendid medieval church. Also close by is another grand ecclesiastical building, Hartland Abbey, dating from the 12thC (1400-1730 Wed., May-Sep.; also Sun., July-Sep. £2.50, child 5-15 £1.25).

Helford: 20 miles west of Penzance. Pop: 265 (inc. Manaccan). This pretty riverside hamlet is the perfect place just to sit and watch the river flow, ideally from the terrace of the popular Shipwright's Arms. You will have to park half a mile away but the walk is worth it. In order to appreciate fully the beauty of the river and such places as Frenchman's Creek, Manderley, Porth Navas and Durgan you will have to take a boat from Falmouth. If you cross the river here by the ferry, keep an eye out for Morgawr – Cornwall's answer to the Loch Ness Monster!

Helston: 13 miles west of Falmouth. Pop: 8000. The market town for The Lizard peninsula (see **A–Z**), Helston is famous for its Furry (or Flora) Dance (see **Events**). Spectators are invited to join in the last dance and most do so, turning the town centre into a huge party area (the name 'furry' is thought to derive from the Cornish word 'fer', meaning 'fair'). Aside from this, Helston is a charming stannary town (see **Mining**)  and well worth a visit. Both Cross St and Coinagehall St contain listed Georgian and older dwellings, including the incongruously thatched Blue Anchor Inn which stills brews its own beer. Off these streets narrow alleyways open almost immediately onto gloriously verdant countryside. Don't miss the Folk Museum, a splendid collection of local bygones housed in the impressive stone halls of the old butter market (1030-1300, 1400-1630 Mon., Tue., Thu.-Sat.; 1030-1200 Wed. Free).

Ilfracombe: Pop: 10,500. This old-fashioned resort is north Devon's most popular holiday spot. Aside from its harbour area it has little character, but boat trips, nearby beaches and various attractions draw the crowds. The nearest sands are the curious Tunnel beaches, quarried under the rocky coast to form a safe, sheltered bathing and rock-pool area (60p, child 30p). The main historical interest is Chambercombe Manor, a predominantly Elizabethan house set in a peaceful, secluded valley, a mile or so from town (1030-1630 Mon.-Fri., 1400-1630 Sun., Easter-Sep. £2, OAP £1.50, child 5-15 £1). There is a Victorian Week festival in June, when townspeople turn back the clock a century.

Kingsbridge: 5 miles north of Salcombe. Pop: 4200. This old market town lies at the mouth of the estuary. Like Totnes, Kingsbridge rises along a steep, narrow High St. It boasts a colonnaded 16thC shambles of shops, a fine 13thC church and a peculiarly shaped town-hall clock tower (19thC). Further on is the splendid Cookworthy Museum of Rural Life in South Devon, one of the county's finest collections, with excellent displays to interest everyone (1000-1700 Mon.-Sat., Easter-Sep.; 1030-1600 Mon.-Fri., Oct. £1, OAP/child 50p, family £2.75).

Lamorna Cove: 6 miles south of Penzance. Pop: 150. Lamorna is famous as one of west Cornwall's most beautiful wooded valleys, with trees and wild flowers running down into a small sandy cove. In and around the valley are several pottery and arts and crafts shops, as well as the Lamorna Wink Pub with its collection of nautical memorabilia. A mile west stand two ancient stone circles: the 19 Merry Maidens and, on the other side of the road, the 15 Pipers, all petrified, according to legend, for dancing on the Sabbath.

Land's End: See CORNWALL-WHAT TO SEE 4.

Launceston: 20 miles northwest of Plymouth. Pop: 6100. Formerly the capital of Cornwall, Launceston spirals spectacularly around a steep hill and is crowned by what remains of its motte-and-bailey castle (EH 1000-1800 Easter-Sep., 1000-1600 Oct.-Easter. 95p, OAP 75p, child 5-16 45p). The commanding views make the climb well worthwhile. The South Gate is the last survivor of the medieval walls and now holds a gallery of hand-painted glass. Almost as old is the fine church of St. Mary Magdalene with its delicately carved granite exterior. High St, Church St and Angel Hill all boast good shopping and several fine old buildings. Don't miss the elegant Lawrence House (NT) on Castle St, home to the local museum (1030-1230, 1430-1630 Mon.-Fri., April, May, Sep., Oct.; 1030-1630 Mon.-Fri., June-Aug. Free; donations invited).

Lizard, The: The Lizard is a flat, weather-beaten peninsula, famous for its tiny coves, remote fishing villages, the extraterrestrial satellite dishes of Goonhilly (particularly atmospheric by night) and the unique rock/mineral serpent which gives the peninsula its name. The following are particularly notable (travelling clockwise): Trelowarren House (see CORNWALL-WHAT TO SEE 2); Goonhilly Earth Station (see CORNWALL-WHAT TO SEE 2); St. Keverne, an outstanding church, the largest in the region, with splendid shipwreck memorials; Coverack, an unspoiled fishing village sitting high above a working harbour; Cadgwith, The Lizard's prettiest fishing village, wedged tightly into a small, narrow cove with 1-in-4 hills dotted with idyllic thatched cottages; Kynance Cove, where the cliffs are some of Cornwall's most spectacular (see CORNWALL-BEACHES 3); Mullion, a small village boasting a beautiful 15thC church and dropping down steeply to a pretty harbour; Gunwalloe, a tiny fishing hamlet with a 15thC church and a lovely, golden-sand cove; and Lizard Point and Village, the most southerly spot in Britain and an uninspiring tourist honeypot, redeemed only by the views and the craft-working of serpentine rock into ornaments. Also in the vicinity just to the north and worth making an effort to see are Gweek's Cornish Seal Sanctuary (see CORNWALL-WHAT TO SEE 2), Helford (see A-Z), Helston (see A-Z) and Porthleven.

LANDS
END
1991

NEW YORK 3147   JOHN O'GROATS 874

SCILLIES 28
ONGSHIPS LIGHTHOUSE 1½

AUCKLAND 12207
9TH MAY

LANDS END

Looe: 18 miles east of St. Austell. Pop: 4500. This popular, picturesque fishing port and resort is bisected into East and West by the harbour river. East Looe is the centre of the tourist activity, with a busy shopping street and a good, sandy beach. Fore St, though not unattractive, is very commercialized. Off here are several streets with 'Chapel' or 'Market' in their names; this is the oldest part of town where charming, unspoiled alleyways of old mariners' cottages are disturbed only by some good-looking up-market restaurants (Surcouf on Lower Chapel St is especially recommended). The Old Guildhall Museum, dating from the 16thC, is worth a look (1000-1900 Sun.-Fri. 60p, child 30p). Boat trips run to Polperro, Fowey, Mevagissey and Plymouth (£5-8 by speedboat, £14-15 by sailboat; inc. coffee and lunch) and Looe is famous for its fishing trips, most notably for shark (£13 for an all-day trip) but also for conger and mackerel (£5-6 per trip). West Looe is mostly residential and has a pretty square just by St. Nicholas Church. See **CORNWALL-BEACHES 4**.

Lundy: 23 miles northwest of Bideford. Pop: 17. This windswept piece of granite is famous for its colourful feathered inhabitants which led the Norse to christen it Lundy (meaning 'Puffin') Island. It is also well known for its inhospitable climatic conditions and its consequent frequent appearances on shipping warnings. Once a pirate hideaway, it is now administered by the National Trust and features the remains of a medieval castle, the Old Light House, a hotel, a pub-cum-shop, a church, a tearoom, a farm and a display on the island's history, wildlife and conservation. If you enjoy bird-watching, visit between May and July when the puffins nest at Jenny's Cove. Lundy is only 3 miles long by half a mile wide but it is well worth a trip if you want to escape from 20thC life for the day. The MS *Oldenburg* runs from Bideford (all year) and Ilfracombe (summer season only). The journey takes 2 hours (£28, child under 17 half-price; booking advisable. Tel: 0237-477676 for Bideford, 0271-863001 for Ilfracombe).

Lydford: 8 miles south of Okehampton. Pop: 1900. This lovely, unspoiled village, famous for its gorge (see **DEVON-WHAT TO SEE 4**), also boasts a sturdy medieval keep (always open. Free) and a fine 15thC church. The excellent village pub is also of historical note and displays

1000-year-old pennies from the reign of Ethelred II. After seeing the gorge, carry on a little further to Brent Tor, a steep hill some 1100 ft above sea level. It is crowned by a weather-beaten 13thC church which stands in splendid isolation and affords superb 360° moorland views.

Lynmouth & Lynton: 17 miles west of Ilfracombe. Pop: 1600. High above these twin villages, Exmoor suddenly ends and comes plunging down Countisbury Hill at a gradient of 1 in 4, scattering lush, sheltered valleys behind the tall trees. It is easy to see why the Victorians called this area Little Switzerland. Lynmouth sits at the foot of the incline, with a pretty harbour and riverside fishing, as well as several cafés to service coach parties. You can visit the Brass Rubbing & Hobbycraft Centre and the beautiful Glen Lyn Gorge (0900-1730. £1.50, OAP/child 75p). Lynmouth is connected with Lynton, perched 600 ft directly above, by an amazing water-powered cliff railway which skates up the 1-in-1.75 gradient at an alarmingly rapid rate. Stand on the outside platform for the best views and speed sensation. At the top just by the railway is a good café. Take the signs via North Walk to the Valley of the Rocks (about a mile) and you will be rewarded with some of this coast's most breathtaking scenery. The valley is a spectacular collection of bizarrely weathered rock formations rejoicing in names like The Devil's Cheesewring. The road winds back down to Lynmouth, passing elegant Victorian and Edwardian houses. See **DEVON-EXCURSION 3.**

Mevagissey: 6 miles south of St. Austell. Pop: 2300. This once-lovely fishing village has become so touristy that its charms have almost disappeared. Tawdry souvenir shops, fast-food stalls and swarming crowds now dominate the harbour and choke the narrow streets. To escape the melee, ascend Up-Along St past the colour-washed cottages and enjoy the fine view. Just below is the local museum, a wonderful collection housed in an atmospheric 18thC workshop (1100-1700 Mon.-Fri., 1100-1600 Sat., 1400-1600 Sun. 30p). Remy's charming tearoom and the basic, smoky Fountain Inn are two notable refreshment oases.

Mining: Tin has been mined in Cornwall for over 1000 years and during the late 18th most of the 19thC the area led the world in the production of tin and copper. In 1870 there were 300 tin mines in Cornwall but by 1896, with the discovery of huge, easily recoverable deposits in Australia and Malaysia, all but a few mines had gone. Today there are no working tin mines left in Cornwall, the last two, at Geevor (see **CORNWALL-WHAT TO SEE 4**) and at South Crofty, having been closed. You can discover the history of Cornish mining and experience something of the terrible conditions in which miners toiled, by taking the underground tours at Geevor Mines, Poldark Mine (see **CORNWALL-WHAT TO SEE 3**) and Morwellham Quay (see **A-Z**). A visit to the Cornish Engines at Pool (see **CORNWALL-WHAT TO SEE 3**) is also recommended and you can see mining relics at local museums in the old stannary towns of Liskeard, Bodmin, Lostwithiel, Truro, Helston and Tavistock. These were the centres where tin was weighed, assayed, stamped and taxed. The most obvious legacies of that bygone age, however, are the derelict, ivy-covered engine houses and chimney stacks which are still dotted all over the county.

Cornwall's other mining industry centres on the extraction of china clay around St. Austell (see **A-Z**). The history of this still-thriving industry can be traced at Wheal Martyn, two miles north of St. Austell (see **CORNWALL-WHAT TO SEE 6**) and at the Shipwreck & Heritage Museum, Charlestown (see **CORNWALL-WHAT TO SEE 6**).

Morwellham Quay: Deep in the heart of the beautiful Tamar Valley, Morwellham is the furthest navigable point up-river and so became the focus of the great copper rush of 1844-59 (see **Mining**). At that time over half a million tons of ore were shipped from here to Plymouth (usually laden into ships at the rate of 50-100 tons per load) and a settlement of around 200 people grew up to service the port. However, as the local mines were exhausted, Morwellham died as quickly as it had been born. In 1970 the trustees of Dartington Hall (see **Dartington**) began the rebuilding of Morwellham and ever since have been restoring the settlement to the way it was in boom times. Port buildings, shops, miners' houses, the quay – complete with a boat – and even the mine have been restored and opened to the public. Quay workers, a cooper, a blacksmith and an assayer all dressed in period costume show off their skills and daily work. The highlight of the visit for most people, however, is the train ride into the old mine. Allow around 6 hours for a visit here. See DEVON-WHAT TO SEE 2.

Mousehole: (pronounced 'Mau-zle') 3 miles south of Penzance. Pop: 2000. This delightful old fishing village has managed to stave off the commercial blight visited upon similar settlements. The oldest building to be found among its winding streets and alleys is the former 16thC manor house in Keigwin St, unmissable with its huge, granite-columned porch. Mousehole's only pub, the Ship Inn, is friendly and full of character, and nearby Annie's is perfect for tea or lunch. Walk up the steep hill to visit the Bird Hospital & Sanctuary (0930-1730. Free) and enjoy the fine harbour view. Just north is Penlee Point where the old lifeboat station has the steepest slipway in England. Adjacent is a memorial garden to the Mousehole crew of the Penlee lifeboat, lost in Dec. 1982.

Newlyn: 2 miles south of Penzance. Pop: 2100. Although Penzance has grown to the very edge of Newlyn, this old fishing settlement still retains its individuality. It is not pretty in the manner of, say, Mousehole, but its small centre has character and, surprisingly for its size, services Cornwall's largest fishing port. Walk around the port for the best views of the fleet which daily lands lobsters, crabs, mackerel and whitebait. Newlyn's other claim to fame is as home to the Newlyn School of Art, formed in the 19thC and still very active today. Their popular works range in style from evocative Victoriana (mostly in Penzance Museum

& Art Gallery; see **Penzance**) to exhibitions of contemporary artists' work in Newlyn Art Gallery, Penzance Rd (1000-1700 Mon.-Sat. Free).

Newquay: Pop: 16,000. The largest and most dedicated resort in north Cornwall, Newquay is famous for its beaches and its surfing. The town occupies a majestic cliff-top position with a traditional old harbour below and adjacent fine, golden sands. Newquay was once a major pilchard-fishing centre, and the Huer's Hut (resembling a tiny, whitewashed

church) on the headland is a reminder of when a lookout used to alert the local fishermen by raising a hue and cry to tell them that shoals had entered the bay. Today, however, tourism is the main industry. Every family-beach facility is provided, and the town's long, rambling main street is crammed with amusement arcades, surfing shacks, fast-food outlets and cheap trinket and souvenir shops. There is plenty to see and do, including the following: Waterworld Aqua Park at Trenance Leisure Park; Time Tunnels, a waxworks-style exhibition of Cornish legends (1000-1500/1600 Sun.-Fri., mid April-Oct.; 1000-2100 daily, early July-early Sep. £1.70, OAP £1.20, child 5-15 85p); Newquay Zoo, newly equipped with a free-flight aviary, lion house, penguin pool and a very good children's zoo (1000-1700. £3.20, OAP/child £2); Trenance Cottages Museum, in tranquil Trenance Gardens, an interesting collection of antiques and curiosities (1000-dusk Easter, May-mid Oct. 60p, OAP/child 40p). Newquay also has a local museum and an aquarium. If you want to escape from the hustle and bustle, visit nearby Crantock, a picturesque village with a lovely church and an old thatched inn.

Nightlife: The only resort towns where there is any real nightlife are Torquay and Newquay, although even here the choice is limited to traditional seaside family-variety shows or fairly unsophisticated discos for the 18-30 crowd. In Exeter and Plymouth the choice is greater, with first-class theatre and music venues. An alternative is to head into the country in search of a good pub. *The Best Pubs in Devon & Cornwall*, by Tim Webb (£4.95), is the best guide for the region. See **Discos**.

Okehampton: 22 miles west of Exeter. Pop: 4000. This busy roadside market town is worth a stop to visit the Museum of Dartmoor Life, set in a charming cobbled courtyard with tearooms, adjacent to the White Hart Hotel (1030-1630 Mon.-Sat., April-June, Sep., Oct.; 1030-1630 daily July-Aug. 50p, child under 16 25p). The romantic ruins of Okehampton Castle lie a mile southwest of here and offer some fine views over the river and Old Deer Park (EH 1000-1800 daily, Easter-Sep.; 1000-1600 Tue.-Sun., Oct.-Easter. £1.30, OAP 95p, child 5-16 65p). Four miles east, at Sticklepath, the Finch Foundry & Museum of Waterpower is highly recommended (1000-1700 Mon.-Sat., Mar., Oct.-22 Dec.; 1000-1700 daily, April-Sep. £1, child 50p).

Ottery St. Mary: 12 miles east of Exeter. Pop: 7000. This pleasant small town is famous for its parish church, the grandest in Devon. Mostly built in the 14thC, its similarity to Exeter Cathedral is due to the fact that the two were built concurrently for the same bishop. There are some good walks around the town; get details from the heritage-trail leaflet which is available from the tourist information centre.

Padstow: 14 miles north of Newquay. Pop: 2800. Padstow has been a major port for centuries and it remains very much a working harbour, giving just a nod to its visitors, with boat trips around the estuary and shark-fishing. The harbour is attractive rather than pretty, and is backed by cobbled alleyways, narrow streets and old-fashioned shops. Opposite the car park on South Quay is a group of 16thC houses with Raleigh Court at its centre; here Sir Walter collected dues in his capacity as Warden of Cornwall. On North Quay see the fine 15thC Abbey House, formerly a nunnery. At midnight on 30 April, the famous Padstow 'Obby

'Oss ceremony begins. The 'oss (horse) and attendants, accompanied by songs, drums and accordions, dance through the streets. A second 'oss joins in later in the day to dance round the maypole and so usher in the summer. Unfortunately, in recent years the ceremony has also ushered in droves of drunkards. For good pub food try the London Inn; fish gourmets should head for the acclaimed Seafood Restaurant at Riverside, off South Quay. Eight miles to the southwest lie the famous Bedruthan Steps – huge, volcanic-rock outcrops scattered on the beach, they are the legendary stepping stones of the giant, Bedruthan.

Paignton: 3 miles south of Torquay. Pop: 35,100. Paignton is the unashamedly cheap 'n' cheerful face of Torbay, with long, sandy, family beaches, a town centre full of garish amusement arcades, 'cheap-eats' and ultra-discount shopping to cater for families on tight budgets. Goodrington Sands is the favourite beach attraction (see **DEVON-BEACHES 2**) and takes in Quaywest Water Park. Even if none of this appeals, Paignton is still a must, if only to board the steam railway (see **DEVON-WHAT TO SEE 7**) or to see the zoo (see **DEVON-WHAT TO SEE 7**).

Pannier Markets: These traditional markets are held in many towns throughout Devon and Cornwall. A pannier is a basket used by small-holders to carry their fruit, vegetables and dairy produce to the market. You can still see pannier markets in Barnstaple (see **A-Z**), Bideford (see **A-Z**), Dartmouth (see **A-Z**), Tavistock (see **A-Z**) and Totnes (see **A-Z**).

Penzance: Pop: 20,000. More of a provincial centre than a holiday resort, Penzance's featureless promenade belies the town's historical and cultural heritage. The oldest part is the area around Chapel St and New St, between the promenade and Market Jew St, the main street. There are no buildings older than 1595, thanks to the town's destruction by the real 'Pirates of Penzance', but Chapel St is full of 17th-19thC architectural gems, including the extravagant Egyptian House (c.1835). Don't miss the Maritime Museum (see **CORNWALL-WHAT TO SEE 4**). There are also several eating houses, a dozen antique shops, the locally famous Admiral Benbow Inn (note the 'smuggler' on the roof) and the Turk's Head, the town's oldest pub. The charming Abbey Lane runs off Chapel St, down to the quay. This is still very much a working-dock area and is home to the National Lighthouse Centre Museum (1000-1800. £2, OAP/child 5-16 £1). Walk back towards the promenade past the splendid 1930s Jubilee Bathing Pool and up Regent's Terrace to Morrab Gardens. Across Morrab Rd is the Penzance Museum & Art Gallery, notable for its collection of Newlyn School (see **Newlyn**) paintings (1030-1630 Mon.-Fri., 1030-1230 Sat. 50p, OAP/child 25p May-Oct., free Nov.-April). Back in the centre of town, across Market Jew St, lie Causequayhead and Bread St. The former is full of character, with old-fashioned shops, while the latter is a centre for arts and crafts, with another seven antique shops and galleries. For more details, pick up a town-trail leaflet from the tourist information centre at the harbour.

Plymouth: Pop: 245,000. The largest city in the region, Plymouth divides neatly into three principal areas: the Hoe (meaning 'high hill'), the Barbican and the modern centre of town. It is best to start exploring from the Hoe, immortalized by Drake at his sighting of the Armada, as a visit to The Dome on the Hoe is the best possible introduction to Plymouth. For an even better view over Plymouth Sound, climb the 93 steps of the displaced lighthouse, Smeaton's Tower. Away to your left is the imposing 17thC Royal Citadel fortress (no entry) and beside it is one of the West Country's best aquariums (1000-1800. £1, child 50p). Walk down the hill beside the Citadel and you will be in the Barbican, Plymouth's fascinating old town. The seafaring heritage here is ubiquitous, with the Island House, the building

where the passengers of the *Mayflower* spent their last night in England in 1620 before sailing from the Mayflower Steps a few yards away, and a host of plaques commemorating other historic voyages. The Barbican is chock-a-block with touristy craft shops, antique shops, warehouses, galleries and even a palmist. New St, built in 1581, is the oldest street here and contains the Elizabethan House Museum (1000-1300, 1400-1730 Tue.-Sat., 1400-1700 Sun., Easter-Sep.; 1000-1630 Tue.-Sat., 1000-1400 BH Mon., Oct.-Easter. 65p, child 15p), near the Elizabethan Garden (0900-1700. Free), and two atmospheric restaurants, the Palace Vaults and Green Lanterns. The only real pub left in the Barbican is the rather seedy Dolphin, though the Wine Lodge and the distillery (where Plymouth Gin is still produced) are both worth a visit.

The modern centre is a short walk from here; en route you will pass the excellent Merchants' House Museum and arrive at the main thorough-fare, Royal Parade, housing the fine Theatre Royal, tourist information centre, Guildhall, St. Andrew's Church and the Prysten House. The large, concrete, pedestrianized area across the road was built after the Blitz destroyed the old centre, and it holds the most comprehensive shopping complex in the region. The only oasis in this grey desert is the excellent City Museum & Art Gallery. See **DEVON-WHAT TO SEE 2**.

Polperro: 4 miles west of Looe. Pop: 920. For many people this is the most picturesque fishing village in Cornwall and despite its hordes of visitors it has resisted the temptations of fast food, kept visitors' cars out of the centre and retains much of the atmosphere of a working fishing village, albeit a showpiece one. Colour-washed cottages line the sides of the narrow, creek-like harbour and some houses literally form part of the sea wall. There are several interesting old higgledy-piggledy build-ings; look out for the House on Props and Couch's Great House and the house of Dr Jonathan Couch (opposite each other). The steep Warren is famed for a charming, shell-adorned fisherman's cottage and continues upwards to join a scenic 2-mile walk to Talland Bay. Polperro's preoc-cupation with free-trading is traced in a good Museum of Smuggling (1000-1830 Easter-Oct. £1, child 60p). The Land of Legend & Model Village features animated models (1030-1830 mid Mar.-mid July, mid Sep.-Oct.; 1030-2130 mid July-mid Sep. £1, OAP/child 60p). Polperro

is well served by restaurants; try the Kitchen (on the way in to the village), the Captain's Cabin or the food in the atmospheric Blue Peter pub.

Port Isaac: 9 miles southwest of Tintagel. Pop: 900. This charming, uncommercialized fishing village clusters tightly around a natural harbour with whitewashed cottages climbing steeply to either side. In high season visitors' cars are banned from its labyrinthine streets, so preserving a peaceful atmosphere. There are no visitor attractions or tourist shops and because of its relative isolation far fewer holiday-makers are seen here than in many other better-known Cornish fishing villages. The terrace of the Golden Lion is a perfect place to rest awhile before visiting the adjacent cove of Port Gaverne. See **CORNWALL-EXCURSION**.

Redruth: 15 miles southwest of Newquay. Pop: 10,200. No more than a name on the A 30 to most holiday-makers, Redruth was once the capital of Cornish mining (see **A-Z**). All that now remains is the Tolgus Tin Stream Museum in town, the Cornish Engines at nearby Pool (see **CORNWALL-WHAT TO SEE 3**) and the silent, ivy-covered chimneys of derelict engine houses. The town is not worth a detour but if you are in search of refreshment with a view, Carn Brea Castle, standing unmissably above Redruth, is the perfect spot. Originally built in the Middle Ages, it is now a restaurant and tearoom and enjoys one of the most spectacular sites in the West Country (tel: 0209-218358; closed Mon.).

Wheal Coates, St. Agnes

St. Agnes: 11 miles southwest of Newquay. Pop: 2000. Formerly a
mining village (St. Anne in the *Poldark* novels), St. Agnes now attracts
surfers and families who pour down the hill to Trevaunance Cove (see
CORNWALL-BEACHES 2). There are cottages on the hillside, most spectacularly those on the amazingly steep and picturesque Stippy Stappy
Lane. Just south of St. Agnes Head is one of Cornwall's most pho-
tographed engine-house remains – Wheal Coates, standing in splendid,
silent isolation, framed by a dramatic coastal backdrop.

St. Austell: Pop: 36,000 (area). The centre of St. Austell is an ugly,
modern development redeemed only by its beautiful 15thC Holy Trinity
church. Three miles east, at Biscovey (signposted 'St. Blazey'), are the
Mid Cornwall Craft Galleries (1000-1700 Mon.-Sat. Free). The St.
Austell area is famous for its great white china-clay slag heaps, visible
from several miles, and known as the Cornish Alps. The Wheal Martyn
museum (see **CORNWALL-WHAT TO SEE 6**) is the best place to learn about
the process of china-clay production. You can then continue the 'trail'
by visiting the unspoiled 200-year-old dock village of Charlestown from
where the clay is still shipped today.

St. Germans: 11 miles west of Plymouth. Pop: 2300. This delightful
village boasts a charming group of Tudor almshouses and one of the
county's best parish churches. Don't miss the carved-stone Norman arch
at the west front or the splendid Eliot Memorial by Rysbrack. Quay Rd
runs down to an idyllic riverside scene comprising a boathouse, swans
and yachts on the reedy Tamar, all framed by a sturdy, 13-arch viaduct.

St. Ives: 6 miles north of Penzance. Pop: 6000. For many people St.
Ives is Cornwall's best all-round resort. The attractive harbour is sur-
rounded by four golden beaches (see **CORNWALL-BEACHES 2**) and the old
town has much of historic interest and a considerable artistic heritage.
There are over 20 galleries in town, chief among these being the St.
Ives Society of Artists at the Sloop Market (1000-1630 Mon.-Sat., Mar.-
early Nov., Dec. 20p, child free). In addition to traditional crafts and
paintings, St. Ives is strong on modern art, with the Barbara Hepworth
Museum renowned for its sculptures (1000-1730 Mon.-Sat, summer;

1000-1630 Mon.-Sat., winter. 50p, OAP/child 25p), and a branch of the Tate Gallery is due to open in 1992/93. When you've had enough of art there is a good local museum (1000-1700 mid May-Oct. 50p, child 30p). The most attractive area of the old town is the maze of narrow streets and tiny fishermen's cottages around the Digey, off Fore St. Fish St boasts St. Ives' oldest house. The grassy Island is a good place for bird-spotting and is ablaze with colour in early summer. Don't miss the tiny chapels of St. Nicholas, on the Island, or St. Leonard's, at the harbour, as well as the fine 15thC church of St. Ia in town. If you have time, take the short but scenic train ride from Porthminster to St. Erth.

St. Mawes: 18 miles southwest of St. Austell. Pop: 1100. A popular but relaxed sailing centre which lacks the commercialized beaches and other 'family amenities' that might disturb its refined serenity. You can see most of it by parking at the bottom of the hill and walking up to its castle, built as an artillery battery by Henry VIII in the 1540s and very similar to Pendennis Castle across the water at Falmouth (EH 1000-1800 Easter-Sep., 1000-1600 Oct.-Easter. 95p, OAP 75p, child 5-16 45p). The steep lanes off the main street contain several charming old cottages. The Rising Sun serves good bar food.

St. Michael's Mount: 4 miles east of Penzance. By day this imposing castle-island dominates St. Michael's Bay, and by night its moonlit silhouette is Cornwall's most magical sight. Its foundation and history follow that of its famous French cousin, Mont St. Michel. The Mount was granted to the Benedictine abbey of Mont St. Michel in the 11thC and in 1135 a church was founded at its summit. The Mount developed from a place of pilgrimage into an important coastal defence which last saw action in the 17thC during the Civil War. Since 1659 it has been owned by the same family, who still live here, though the administration is now in the hands of the National Trust. A causeway links the island to Marazion at low tide, and a rowing boat takes you across at other times. The little island is a delight to visit, with its charming Victorian harbour settlement, its steep, cobbled castle walk which affords wonderful views, and its castle and chapel, part medieval and with beautiful Georgian decor. See **CORNWALL-WHAT TO SEE 3**.

St. Michael's Mount

Salcombe: 22 miles southeast of Plymouth. Pop: 2450. As you descend into Salcombe, tantalizing views of tiny, golden beaches set around a pretty harbour appear in and out of the trees. This is one of the largest yachting centres in England and certainly one of the most attractive. Park at the far end of town by the ice-cream factory, and walk back past the old wharf houses, still used by boat makers and marine engineers. The centre is quaint and old-fashioned with weatherboarded, tile-hung houses and shops and a distinct lack of amusement arcades. For refreshment, with a view of the flotilla, try the terrace of the Wardroom or the Ferry Inn. Clare's is recommended for a romantic evening meal. Although Salcombe is not considered a beach resort, North Sands, South Sands (with a water-skiing and windsurfing school) and Splat Cove are a short walk along Cliff Rd, and ferries will take you across the harbour to four other beaches (as well as Kingsbridge; see **A-Z**). Hope Cove, 3 miles east, is also worth a visit, although its sand is covered at high tide. A mile and a half southwest, at Sharpitor, is Overbecks Museum and Gardens. The lovely gardens have a spectacular estuary view and the elegant Edwardian House holds a fine collection of local maritime and natural-history artefacts (NT Gardens 1000-2000 or dusk; museum 1200-1700 April-Oct. Garden £1.80, child 5-17 half price; plus museum £2.60).

Sidmouth: 4 miles east of Exeter. Pop: 11,800. Sidmouth has been a favourite resort since it gained royal patronage in the early 19thC and much of its old-world charm remains today. The seafront is particularly attractive in summer, with its Regency architecture enhanced by glorious floral displays. Many 19th and early-20thC buildings have also been retained, with delightful, old-fashioned shop fronts in the thriving centre. The town's immaculate housekeeping extends to the beaches, with two coveted Blue Flags (see **DEVON-BEACHES 2**). Sidmouth shakes off its sedate atmosphere for one week each year during the International Festival of Folk Arts (see **Events**), when top-quality singers, dancers and artists from all over the world perform at over 500 staged events, with almost as many again played impromptu (often as free previews) on the Esplanade, in pubs, parks and all over town.

South Molton: 11 miles east of Barnstaple. Pop: 3600. There is plenty of interest in and around this bustling market town. The focus is the square and town hall, containing the local museum (1030-1300, 1400-1600 Tue.-Thu., Fri.; 1030-1230 Wed. & Sat., Mar.-Nov. Free). Around the square are antique and craft shops, and the towering 15thC church of St. Mary Magdalene is well worth a look. On Thu. there is a market in the 19thC pannier-market hall (see **Pannier Markets**). The town's most popular attraction is the Quince Honey Farm (see **DEVON-WHAT TO SEE 6**), while Hancock's Devon Cider Mill, 3 miles south of town, is also worth a visit (0900-1300, 1400-1730 Mon.-Sat. £1.30, child 75p).

Sport: Spectator sports in the area include the following:
Cricket – Devon CC (minor counties league): Torquay, Sidmouth, Exmouth, Budleigh Salterton.
Football – Plymouth Argyle, Home Park, Plymouth; Torquay Utd, Plainmoor, Torquay; Exeter City, St. James Park, Exeter.
Horse Racing – Newton Abbot; Devon & Exeter Racecourse, near Haldon, Exeter.
Speedway – Exeter Falcons, County Ground, St. Thomas, Exeter.
Stock-car Racing – Newton Abbot racecourse (Wed.).
Participator sports are as follows:
Golf – Municipal courses and private clubs open to non-members:

St. Enodoc (near Wadebridge), Royal North Devon Club, Westward Ho!; West Cornwall Golf Club, Lelant (near St. Ives). The following clubs participate in golfing holidays: Bude & North Cornwall Golf Club, Bude; Carlyon Bay Golf Club (near St. Austell); Falmouth Golf Club; Bigbury Golf Club, Thurlestone. Tourist information centres carry a free booklet, *Learn to Play Golf*, and will give you details of your nearest course.

Fishing – Shark and deep-sea angling are available from several ports, including Penzance, Falmouth, St. Ives, Mousehole, Looe and Padstow. There is coarse fishing at Porth (near Newquay).

Horse Riding – St. Ives, St. Just, Sennen, Polpever (near Looe), Truro, Launceston, Newquay, Davidstowe (near Camelford), St. Blazey (near St. Austell), Okehampton, Widecombe-in-the-Moor, Lynton, Lydford. Prices are around £6 per hr, £25 per half day.

Tennis – Sunnybanks Tennis Farm at Fletcher's Bridge near Bodmin is a major centre but public courts are widely available. See **Water Sports**.

Tavistock: 14 miles north of Plymouth. Pop: 9300. The wealth and history of Tavistock have been linked closely in turn with its once-great abbey and then with local copper mining (see **A-Z**). The abbey gateway survives as part of the town hall (on Bedford Sq.), and other remains include The Misericord, or infirmary dining hall – now a chapel (opposite), Betsey Grimbal's Tower (next to the Bedford Hotel on Plymouth Rd) and part of the cloisters in the yard of the fine 15thC church of St. Eustace. There is a good local-history exhibition at the tourist information centre in the town hall. Today Tavistock is a lively market centre with a busy pannier market (see **A-Z**) behind the town hall every Fri. (antiques, crafts and bric-a-brac are sold on Tue. and Wed.). The Goose Fair, held on the second Wed. in Oct., draws large crowds.

Teignmouth: 8 miles north of Torquay. Pop: 13,300. Teignmouth has a distinctive seafront, with a long, sandy beach flanked by grass-topped red cliffs and bisected by its pier. Once a fashionable resort, it is now a quiet retreat for families and elderly holiday-makers. The town exudes a faded charm, particularly around its small harbour area. Nearby at the pretty village of Shaldon, the Shaldon Wildlife Trust Zoo is a breeding centre for rare species of small mammals, exotic birds and reptiles (1000-1830 Easter-Sep.; 1000-1600 Oct.-Easter. £1.95, OAP/child £1.20). Every Wed. in summer Shaldon stages a '1785 Day', with period costume, stalls, crafts and evening entertainment.

Theatre: The main Devon theatre is the Theatre Royal, Plymouth, which stages major national productions. Also in town, the Athaeneum stages top-quality amateur performances, while the Barbican is a dance venue. Exeter also has good performance venues in the Northcott Theatre and the Devon Arts Centre. The most famous Cornish venue is the splendidly situated Minack Theatre, carved out of the rock in Greek-amphitheatre style and perched precariously on the cliff top above Porthcurno (see **CORNWALL-WALK**). Performances include popular musicals, drama and classics, and are staged from late May to mid Sep. Take a cushion and some warm clothing! You can also visit the theatre and its exhibition centre (1000-1730 April-Oct.; closes 1600 Oct. & 1200-1430 on matinee days; tel: 0736-810694. £1.20, OAP 80p, child 50p). There are also open-air theatres at Upton Cross, near Liskeard, and at Silverlands, near Chudleigh. One-off performances are also held at Mount Edgcumbe, Plymouth and at some National Trust properties.

Tintagel: 17 miles southwest of Bude. Pop: 1600. The pretty village which is the legendary site of King Arthur's castle has been commercialized almost to the point of parody. Pilgrims should start at King Arthur's Great Hall, a huge (modern) stone building with an electronic theatre that recounts the Arthurian legend (1000-1700 April-mid Oct. £1.75, child 85p, family £5). Tintagel Castle (see **CORNWALL-WHAT TO SEE 1**) lies beyond the far end of High St and is reached by a 15-min rocky descent or landrover ride for the less physically able. Disappointingly for some, it is no more than a fragmentary ruin and dates from the 13thC (700 years post-Arthur), with no interpretation of the legend. The setting, however, is fit for a king. Back in High St, be sure not to miss The Old Post Office (see **CORNWALL-WHAT TO SEE 1**). See **CORNWALL-EXCURSION**.

Tiverton: 15 miles north of Exeter. Pop: 17,000. This busy crossroads market town is worth a stop to see the 15thC parish church of St. Peter and the excellent local museum (1030-1630 Mon.-Sat., mid April-Sep. Free). The castle contains a Civil War armoury and a clock collection but may be missed if you are short of time. The tourist information centre in Phoenix Lane produces a good town-trail brochure.

Topsham: 3 miles south of Exeter. Pop: 4650. This charming riverside port boasts so many historic buildings that the whole town is designated a conservation area. The Strand's fine houses include Topsham Museum, a 17thC merchant's house featuring maritime exhibits (1400-1700 Mon., Wed., Sat., Feb.-Nov.; also Sun. Aug., Sep. 60p, child 35p). Topsham is well blessed, too, with good pubs – try the Passage Inn on the Strand, the Globe Hotel, or the 16thC Bridge Inn on the River Clyst, just outside town. Topper's Restaurant is also recommended.

Torquay: Pop: 120,000. Torquay is the second most visited British seaside town after Blackpool, with a popularity founded on long, safe, sandy beaches and a climate mild enough to grow palm trees and so encourage an exotic, Mediterranean image. That Riviera touch is most apparent at the marina where the international yacht set gather and the ambience is as Gallic as Gauloises. Elsewhere in the town centre and along the promenade the aroma is the all pervasive vinegar 'n' chips of the not-so-chic, typically British resort. Facilities for a family holiday are good, however, come rain or shine. Kent's Cavern, the Model Village and Bygones are the best of Torquay's many attractions, and with Brixham and Paignton so close, plus castles at Berry Pomeroy (EH 1000-1800 Easter-Sep. £1.30, concessions 95p, child 65p. Ruins only) and Compton (NT 1000-1215, 1400-1700 April-Oct. £2, child 5-17 half price), there is no shortage of sights. Shopping is also well catered for, with new developments at Fleet Walk and the elegant Edwardian Pavilion. Good food and drink can be found, though it is not readily

apparent, and in addition to those places recommended in **DEVON-RESTAURANTS** you may like to try The Hole in the Wall pub on the Strand, and Maggie's restaurant at Park Lane. Nightlife is plentiful, with several discos (see **A-Z**), variety-show venues and a new, high-tech ten-pin bowling centre. Market day is Mon. (on the ring road).

Suburbs which also merit a visit are St. Marychurch and Cockington. The former, close to the Model Village, is best visited on a Thu. evening (1930-2130 summer) when the clock is turned back to the Victorian age and shopkeepers dressed in period costume, and a brass band and dancers fill the old-fashioned main shopping street. Cockington is a beautiful picture-postcard village, so close to the centre of Torquay that it could almost have been purpose-built for tourists. The best time to see it is in the early morning while it is still peacefully empty of other visitors. The 270-acre wood-land-and-lakeside grounds of Cockington Court are ideal for walking, before you repair to the Drum Inn for refreshments. You can walk to Cockington from the centre of Torquay (a mile away) or take a pony and trap (around £8 per person).

Totnes: 8 miles west of Torquay. Pop: 3300. This ancient, picturesque town is situated on the River Dart and boat trips run from the steamer quay at the bottom end of the town. Park here and walk up the steep, claustrophobic High St, crowned by its Tudor East Gate. There are several 16th and 17thC merchants' houses lining this attractive street,

with the finest being The Elizabethan House, beautifully converted to hold the local museum (1030-1300, 1400-1700. 60p, child 25p). The Bogan House at no. 43 is also a museum, displaying the Devonshire Collection of Period Costume (1100-1700 Mon.-Fri., 1400-1700 Sun., Spring BH-Sep. Tel: 0803-862423 for admission charges). Turn right just before the East Gate arch, up Rampart Walk, and visit the splendidly preserved 16thC Guildhall (1000-1300, 1400-1700 Mon.-Fri. 30p, child 15p). Further up High St you will see why Totnes calls itself the 'natural health capital of the West Country', with a plethora of wholefood shops and restaurants (try the excellent Willow). To the right is the 12thC motte-and-bailey Totnes Castle (EH 1000-1800 Easter-Sep., 1000-1600 Tue.-Sun., Oct.-Easter. 95p, concessions 75p, child 5-16 45p). Turn left down Leechwell St to the picturesque 17thC Kingsbridge Inn and to the left of the pub Leechwell Lane will lead you to an ancient well. The best time to visit Totnes is on a Tue. in summer, when the town traders dress in Elizabethan costume and you can join a free guided tour starting from the bridge at the bottom of the hill (meet 1430). The antiques and pannier market (see **A-Z**) on Fri. is also worth a visit. The town also has a motor museum, at the steamer quay, featuring sports and racing cars (1000-1750 Easter-Oct. Tel: 0803-862777 for admission charges).

Tourist Information: All towns and most villages which receive tourists have an official tourist information centre. They will give general advice on where to go, sell you maps and are a good place to pick up leaflets and free local information. All the major (and many minor) centres offer an accommodation-booking service. For advance information, contact the West Country Tourist Board at their head office: Trinity Court, 37 Southernhay East, Exeter EX1 1QS, tel: 0392-76351.

Tours: Devon and Cornwall are well served by coach tours which visit most major towns and sights. Grey Cars of Torquay go all over Devon picking up from Torquay, Paignton and Brixham, and Western National, departing from Newquay, boasts Cornwall's most extensive programme. Several other operators pick up from major centres, such as Ilfracombe and Penzance. Expect to pay around £4-6 for a day's outing. However, if you want to get away from the tourist honey pots and see some of the 'real' Cornwall, join a Master Tours coach at Penzance for their 'Industrial Heritage', 'Wildlife & Environment', '*Poldark*', 'Art & the Landscape' or 'Antiquities' excursions; tickets are available from Penzance tourist information centre (Mar.-Oct. £9.50). See **Boat Trips**.

Truro: Pop: 19,000. Truro is the county town of Cornwall, its centre dominated by its neo-Gothic 19thC cathedral (see **CORNWALL-WHAT TO SEE 6**). The town prospered in the 18th-19thC from mining profits and it retains a good Georgian architectural legacy, notably in River St, Lemon St, Princes St and Walsingham Place. Pydar St has several early houses converted to retail outlets and is the principal thoroughfare of the county's main shopping centre. There are several good refreshment options: try the tearoom of the excellent County Museum (see **CORNWALL-WHAT TO SEE 6**), the trendy Brasserie (shop/restaurant) opposite, or the ancient setting of Chimes coffee house, by the cathedral. Truro's newest attraction is the Museum of Entertainment at Old Bridge St, with memorabilia from show business and music (1000-1700. £1.50, 95p concessions).

Veryan: 13 miles southeast of Truro. Pop: 500. This charming village is the showpiece of the beautiful Roseland peninsula, and is famous for its five 19thC thatched whitewashed round houses. According to local legend their shape is to keep out the devil, as he needs a north wall to enter a house. There is also a cross on each roof. The parish church has a luxuriant water garden.

Wadebridge: 14 miles northeast of Newquay. Pop: 4800. This market town and port at the head of the Camel estuary is worth a detour. Aside from a good shopping centre, the scenic Camel Trail runs through here (see **Bicycle & Motorcycle Hire**). At nearby Tredinnick is the Cornish Shire Horse Centre (tel: 0841-540276 for details), and the Cornwall Folk Festival takes place in Wadebridge on Aug. bank-holiday weekend.

Walking: Whether you want a scenic afternoon stroll or an energetic long-distance hike you won't have to look far in Devon or Cornwall. The Southwest Way Coastal Path is Britain's longest footpath, winding for 570 miles around the peninsula. The Southwest Way Association produces a guide to the whole path (£2.95) as well as leaflets relating to certain sections (60p each). The National Trust, which owns around one-third of the path, produces similar leaflets which are sold from its shops. Two of the most spectacular sections are the Devon border to Combe Martin, and St. Ives to Penzance, and these are briefly touched on in the walks in the blue section of this book. If you want a guided walk you will find a regular programme at several tourist information centres. Extensive programmes are also run by National Park rangers on Dartmoor and Exmoor. These walks cost from 50p-£1 on Exmoor, 90p-£2 on Dartmoor. If you want to walk the moors by yourself, the tourist information centres have plenty of walking guides and maps, and the helpful staff will also give you advice. Be aware that the weather on the high moors can change suddenly so always take adequate clothing and maps. 'Danger areas' marked on maps of Dartmoor refer to MOD firing ranges and red flags are flown and the ranges marked by boundary posts when firing is in progress. See **DEVON-WALKS, CORNWALL-WALK**.

Water Sports: The following list is a selection of venues and is not intended to be comprehensive:
Canoeing – Tamar Canoe Expedition, tel: 0579-51113, departs from Gunnislake along a 7-mile stretch of the Tamar. No experience

necessary. Easter–mid Sep. £22 per double canoe, £12 per single, no children under 8.

Diving – Brixham, Breakwater Beach; Plymouth, Fort Bovisand Centre; Penzance Sub-Aqua Club, Albert Pier; Polkerrish Divers, St. Eval, near Wadebridge. £60 per one-day course.

Jet-skiing – Saunton Sands; Plymouth, Queen Anne's Battery Marina; Falmouth, Gyllyngvase Beach; St. Ives. £12 per 30 min inc. tuition and equipment.

Parascending – Newquay, St. Ives, Torquay.

Surfing – Offshore Surfing School, Newquay: courses from £15 inc. equipment. Malibu board hire £1.50 per hr, £6 per day; with wet suit £3 per hr, £12 per day. Body boards £2 per hr, £8 per day.

Waterskiing – £55 per boat (max. four people).

Windsurfing – £5 per hr, £10 per half day, £20 per day (inc. wet suit).

Yachting & Sailing clubs – Falmouth, Manaccan, Looe, Marazion, Salcombe, Newton Ferrers, Penzance, St. Mawes, Dartmouth, Exmouth, Torquay, Plymouth. £20 per hr.

There are also major water-sports centres at Mylor Yacht Harbour, Falmouth, and The Harbour, Paignton. Details are available from the West Country Tourist Board's free brochure, *Activity & Leisure Holidays*.

Westward Ho!: 3 miles west of Bideford. Pop: 2100. The romance of Charles Kingsley's eponymous seafaring novel (published 1855) has unfortunately long since deserted Westward Ho!. What you will find today is a very prosaic self-catering resort of chalets, caravans and flats with discount shops and cheap and characterless refreshment places. There is, however, a 3-mile-long golden, sandy beach with good surfing and windsurfing for experienced wave riders and, close by, a good golf course. The adjacent grassy coastal plain and dunes make up Northern Burrows Country Park which has a visitor centre devoted to local ecology. See **DEVON-BEACHES 1**.

What's On: Check local newspapers and tourist information centres (see **A-Z**). *South West Events* is the region's only comprehensive listings magazine (60p monthly from newsagents). Look out also for the following (free from tourist information centres unless otherwise stated):
North Devon Scene (one-off summer magazine; 60p from newsagents); *Exeter Gazette & What's On, Exeter & East Devon Scene* (monthly leaflet); *English Riviera Visitor* (monthly what's on); *Dartmoor Visitor* and *Exmoor Visitor* (one-off summer newspapers); *South Hams Holiday Times* (one-off summer newspaper).
Cornwall Review (monthly newspaper); *What's On in West Cornwall* (monthly magazine).

Widecombe-in-the-Moor: 7 miles west of Bovey Tracey. Pop: 600. This picturesque Dartmoor village of English folk-song fame now attracts Uncle Tom Cobleigh and all by the coachload and in summer its charm is somewhat overwhelmed. Its soaring church, the 'cathedral of the moors', has been a landmark since the 15thC and the National Trust now administers the adjacent Church House (1400-1700 Tue., Thu.,

June–mid Sep. Free). Leave the Old Inn to the coach parties and walk some 200 yd past the church to the Rugglestone Inn, a rare example of a totally unspoiled moorland pub (no food). The famous Widecombe Fair is celebrated on the second Tue. in Sep. and draws large crowds. See **DEVON-EXCURSION 1**.

Woolacombe: 6 miles west of Ilfracombe. Pop: 1250. The sole focus of attention at this old-fashioned resort, popular with families and the elderly, is the attractive beach (see **DEVON-BEACHES 1**). The adjacent village of Mortehoe by contrast offers a medieval church, a good pub (The Ship Aground), a very pleasant tearoom and the interesting Butters wholefood restaurant. Take the short walk to Morte Point, some 200 ft high, for fine views over the coast and headland. Close by is Once Upon a Time, a young children's theme park created by the owners of Watermouth Castle (same opening times as Watermouth Castle; see **DEVON-WHAT TO SEE 1**. £2.60 child, £1.60 adult, £1.35 OAP).

Youth Hostels: Youth hostels in the area are as follows:
Devon – Beer; Bellever, near Postbridge, Dartmoor; Dunsford, north-west Dartmoor; Elmscott, near Hartland; Exeter; Galmpton, near Brixham; Ilfracombe; Instow, near Bideford; Lownard, near Dartington; Lynton; Plymouth; Sharpitor, near Salcombe.
Cornwall – Boscastle; Boswinger, near Gorran, St. Austell Bay; Coverack, the Lizard; Golant, near Fowey; Newquay; Pendennis Castle, Falmouth; Penzance; Perranporth, near St. Agnes; St. Just-in-Penwith, near Land's End; Tintagel; Treyarnon Bay, near Padstow.

Zennor: 6 miles west of St. Ives. Pop: 215. This tiny village, set in some of Cornwall's most rugged and least developed countryside, boasts a fine 12thC church famous for the 16thC carving of a mermaid on one of its bench-ends. If you want to hear the legend of the scaly seductress ask in the Tinner's Arms! A few yards away is the charming old Wayside Museum of domestic and agricultural bygones (1000-1800 Easter-Oct. £1.50, OAP/child £1). This part of Cornwall is known for its Stone Age remains and a mile southeast stands the Zennor Quoit, the largest neolithic chamber tomb (c.3000 BC) in England.

This edition published 1995 by Diamond Books
77–85 Fulham Palace Road, Hammersmith,
London W6 8JB

Text: Paul Murphy
Photography: Portfolios Photography
Electronic Cartography: Susan Harvey Design

First published 1992 Reprinted 1992
Copyright © HarperCollins*Publishers*

Printed in Italy

ISBN 0 261 66593-6